Montaigne's Essais

Nicholas Capaldi
General Editor

Stuart D. Warner
Associate Editor

Vol. 11

PETER LANG
New York • Washington, D.C./Baltimore • Bern
Frankfurt am Main • Berlin • Brussels • Vienna • Oxford

WENDELL JOHN COATS, JR.

Montaigne's Essais

PETER LANG
New York • Washington, D.C./Baltimore • Bern
Frankfurt am Main • Berlin • Brussels • Vienna • Oxford

Library of Congress Cataloging-in-Publication Data
Coats, Wendell John.
Montaigne's Essais / Wendell John Coats, Jr.
p. cm. — (Masterworks in the Western tradition; v. 11)
Includes bibliographical references and index.
1. Montaigne, Michel de, 1533–1592. Essais. I. Title. II. Series.
PQ1643.C56   844'.3—dc22   2003019425
ISBN 0-8204-6316-7
ISSN 1086-539X

Bibliographic information published by **Die Deutsche Bibliothek**.
Die Deutsche Bibliothek lists this publication in the "Deutsche
Nationalbibliografie"; detailed bibliographic data is available
on the Internet at http://dnb.ddb.de/.

Cover design by Sophie Boorsch Appel

The paper in this book meets the guidelines for permanence and durability
of the Committee on Production Guidelines for Book Longevity
of the Council of Library Resources.

© 2004 Peter Lang Publishing, Inc., New York
275 Seventh Avenue, 28th Floor, New York, NY 10001
www.peterlangusa.com

All rights reserved.
Reprint or reproduction, even partially, in all forms such as microfilm,
xerography, microfiche, microcard, and offset strictly prohibited.

Printed in the United States of America

For B.L.C.

Contents

Preface ix

CHAPTER I
Introducing Montaigne and the *Essais* 1

CHAPTER II
Montaigne's Philosophy of Appropriate Living 9

CHAPTER III
Montaigne's Religious Views 60

CHAPTER IV
Montaigne's Political Views 79

CHAPTER V
Bibliographic Essay 90

Concluding Postscript 105

Notes 107

Bibliography 119

Index 123

Preface

This study of Montaigne's *Essais* is intended for general readers as well as academic specialists and should maintain interest for both readerships. Its distinguishing feature as a piece of Montaigne commentary is the attempt to identify a unifying theme throughout the various and ostensibly diverse essays—Montaigne's pursuit of psychic repose through "temporal solipsism"—that is, through living in the present moment insofar as intelligently possible.

Thanks to Nick Capaldi as an editor of the Masterworks series for the opportunity to write this book; to Connecticut College for support during a semester sabbatical leave devoted to this work, and for the 2003 Rash Research Award which was helpful in production of this book; to Ann Hartle for her collegial generosity to a stranger at the inception of this project; to Dirk Held and Pamela Jensen for commentary on parts of the manuscript; to Sharon Moody for daring to type from my script; and to Stanford University Press for permission to quote extensively from the Frame translation. All the usual disclaimers about responsibility for issues of fact and judgment apply. A version of Chapter 2 on Montaigne's "art of living" was presented as a lecture in the Connecticut College *De Litteris II* series in May 2003.

CHAPTER I

Introducing Montaigne and the *Essais*

Michel de Montaigne, the author of the *Essais,* was the first generation of his family to qualify as belonging to the sixteenth-century French military aristocracy *(noblesse d'epée)* by virtue of his grandfather's purchase of the Montaigne estate (near Bordeaux) three generations prior. (Ownership of the estate entailed military obligation to the king of France; membership in the *noblesse d'epée* required that a family had not engaged in commercial trade, except for the sale of estate wine, for at least three generations.[1]) During his lifetime, which included three decades of French religious civil war between Catholics and Protestants (Huguenots), Montaigne served two consecutive terms as mayor of Bordeaux (an office normally reserved for military aristocracy), and also served as a reliable negotiator for kings of France, notably Henry of Navarre, later Henry IV. He also may have seen military combat at close quarters for the Catholic side at his own request; his funeral statue shows him in full armor, and the people of Bordeaux never criticized this as the act of an imposter.[2]

He was raised by a caring father, who saw that he learned Latin before French and had him nursed in a peasant village in order that he gain appreciation for the insights of the "common people." At the age of thirty-eight, following the death of his dear friend, Étienne de la Boétie, he first attempted to retire to his study at Montaigne to write and reflect. Although called to public service, he persisted in this effort, producing the first edition of his *Essais* in 1580, continually revising and expanding them until his death in 1592. The Frame translation of the *Essais,* which I have used for this book, follows the convention of indicating successive textual revisions of the *Essais* through the notation, "A" (earliest), "B," and "C" (latest).³ The *Essais* are organized into three volumes and range in length from less than a page to almost 150 pages. Book I contains fifty-seven generally short essays; Book II, thirty-seven essays, including the very long "Apology for Raymond Sebond"; and Book III, thirteen rather long essays.

Early on, the subject of Montaigne's reflections became himself and his relation to the world. Although the style and length of essays changed over time (the later ones long and more outspoken), how much Montaigne's substantive views (versus his momentary emphases) changed or evolved is a matter of scholarly dispute, characterized in the concluding bibliographic essay of this book. Montaigne's reasons for writing the *Essais* are complex and may have evolved as well. He tells the reader that they were written for private purposes (to explore and console himself; to provide friends and relatives memories of him after he is gone), yet he caused them to be published, continually revised them (including new material to entertain previous readers), and made presents of them to royalty. In my view, it is beyond doubt that Montaigne hoped and expected to have some general effect on his readership then and posthumously, though this was not his overriding purpose in writing the *Essais*. As we shall see, Montaigne eschewed strictly instrumental purposes in most things.

Lively commentary on and criticism of the *Essais* began in Montaigne's own time and continues to this day. The breadth of views in this commentary is engendered in part because Montaigne's meaning in the disparate and ostensibly "rambling" *Essais* is not always clear, and often appears contradictory. The reasons for these apparent contradictions are themselves open to interpretation—a faithful reflection of Montaigne's own internal inconsistency (?), a controlled employment of skeptical rhetorical technique to induce suspension of judgment in the reader (?), the mere surface of a coherent but hidden argument (?), and so on.

The view of the *Essais* presented in this book is meant to encourage a "naive" reading by liberally educated general readers in the interest of gaining an appreciation of Montaigne's approach to the "art of living." *Some* of the issues raised in the secondary literature are important and become interesting when held up against the reader's own analysis of the full meaning of the texts in question. Since one of Montaigne's points is often followed by an apparently contradictory one, secondary literature which adduces scattered quotations to support a particular theme can be misleading. The soundest approach is to read each essay from beginning to end, including the long "Apology for Raymond Sebond," the major subject of this book's chapter on Montaigne's religious views.

Montaigne's subject in the *Essais* is himself, of, and vis-à-vis the world. Although he is impressed with the natural diversity and changeability of the world—human and nonhuman—and distrustful of the limited capacity of human reason and human generalization to grasp and explain this diversity and flux without explaining it away, still, "by accident," in exploring himself he comes upon the more abiding aspects and characteristics of his own personality. For example, he finds that it is the essence of his being to prefer open and extensive communication; that he dislikes cruelty of any sort, even toward dumb animals; that he prefers pursuits of the private realm, such as friendship and conversation, in which people and actions can be taken on their own terms rather than as more instrumental means to future ends; that when he must perform public duties he tries always to do so in "as private a manner as possible," and so on.

At least part of the adventure in reading and studying Montaigne's *Essais* is the attempt to make sustainable generalizations—that is, meaningful and accurate generalizations—about his orientation to living, his "art of living" (a Cartesian phrase for a very anti-Cartesian viewpoint). He tells us that he changes so much from moment to moment that he does not paint his being, but his movement. Yet, if Montaigne were really just a series of instantaneous states of consciousness given continuity merely by being housed in the same mortal coil, readers would quickly lose interest in what he has to say owing to its lack of meaning. And, at any rate, as we've just observed, Montaigne himself begins to see the "ruling pattern" in his own personality, which strives to assert and preserve itself in the face of the internal and external changeability that constantly challenges it.

The approach of this interpretation of Montaigne's *Essais*, then, is a rather formal one (especially in contrast to various postmodernist readings[4]), which looks for patterned meaning in the *Essais*; which presumes that there are criteria for these meanings outside the *Essais* themselves, in at least the phenomenological structure of the world as Montaigne perceived it; and which resists the view that Montaigne's meaning is deeply hidden or disguised as part of some practical or instrumental project, or that his literary *persona* is widely divergent from his actual one. In my view, this approach makes the most coherent sense of the evidence about himself and his views and is the most likely to give us a faithful portrait of Montaigne's own intentions in writing the various essays (a criterion outside the essays themselves).

In this context, the view to which a reading of some of the best secondary literature and a complete re-reading the *Essais* has led, is the following.[5] In spite of differences in emphasis over the decades during which the *Essais* were written and revised, there is evident a fairly consistent approach to the "art of living," that is, living well, appropriately, and happily as a human being immersed in a world of contingencies, internal and external. The first thing to be observed about Montaigne's approach is its goal or general orientation, which is clearly as much repose or tranquillity in the soul (his language) available to us when we accurately match our individual capacities and our general capacities as human beings with what we can realistically achieve in life. (One can imagine, by contrast, other orientations—lives directed above all else to duty, or moral rectitude, or patriotism or military glory, or literary fame, or sensual appetite, or scientific mastery of nature, and so on.)

In combination with other considerations—Montaigne's lack of decisive executive ability, his poor memory, his instinctive candor, the civil war around him, among others—he is led to an appreciation of private life, for it is in private life that it is most appropriate to do things for their own sake—to live in the present moment—and this is the key to psychic repose for Montaigne. Practical and political schemes that require complicated, instrumental planning and scheming and manipulation of men and events force one to live for the future (a very uncertain, alienated future) and do not lend themselves to internal repose. Montaigne appears to believe that only very great individuals (like Alexander and Caesar) can take on grand instrumental projects and *not* be so consumed by them that they are unable to do other things for their own sake.

Another reason why Montaigne eschews complicated instrumental projects is his assessment of the paucity of human intellect and reason (hence his penchant for arguments and tropes of the ancient skeptics). Like St. Augustine (but unlike either the Pyrrhonian and Academic Skeptics), Montaigne appears to believe that the proper focus for the reasoning powers of a creature of body and soul immersed in an earthly flux of time and contingency is human conduct and human meaning. He clearly does not foresee the modern scientific project to master nature through steady and controlled accumulation of "data," nor anticipate its degree of success in this endeavor, though this does *not* mean that his assessment of the ultimate futility of this kind of project (from the standpoint of human repose and psychic harmony) is off the mark. (The answer to that question is not in yet).

Montaigne's assessment of the limited capacities of human reasoning in combination with his insight (borrowed in part from Horace[6] and Seneca) about the importance of living in the present moment, as well as the realization of the flux and changeability of his own personality, lead Montaigne to an appreciation of the ritualistic[7] aspects of life and to a rather conservative approach to the basis for political legitimacy and religious orthodoxy (though, as we shall see, some of his personal views would be considered "progressive" by modern liberalism). Montaigne's religious and political views are a subject of scholarly dispute, with interpretations ranging from the view that he was an atheist and Machiavellian of sorts to the view that he was a religious and political conservative. In between are views that Montaigne's religious and political conservatism was purely instrumental, intended to mollify the effects of the civil war. These controversies are the reason for devoting separate chapters in this study to Montaigne's religious and political views. For the present, suffice it to say that in coming to decisions about religious and political controversy, Montaigne counsels an approach that weights or privileges one's religious and political inheritance, precisely because it is inherited. Also, for the present, it is sufficient to indicate that the interpretation favored here is that Montaigne was sincere in his defense of his inherited Roman Catholic faith and practice, and of the French monarchy; and also sincere in his advocacy (at least for himself) of a private over a public life, and of a truly private life rather than one utilizing time and energy in private for future public or political and social purposes and projects. Montaigne implies that if his *Essais* could have a salutary effect on his civilization, so much the better, but that he was not prepared to craft them with that end constantly in mind.

Another of Montaigne's important and influential themes concerns the cultivation of his own individuality for its own sake, though not in the willful and excessive way characteristic of the subsequent Romantic movement or of Nietzsche's writing. He implies dramatically (by the time and energy he devotes to the project of exploring and essaying himself) that his individuality is important simply for itself and not for the universal characteristics it illustrates or deviates from, though it is reflective of these as well. In the terms of medieval scholastic philosophy, he implies that his particular "existence" is not simply "accident," but an integral part of his "essence," and that this is true of all individuals as particular concretions of body and soul. Thus the importance for Montaigne of an individual learning to belong to himself or herself, of making a life all one's own in conformity with one's "ruling pattern" *(forme maistresse)* against the constraints and impulses of the universal human condition—material, physical, and spiritual—and the contradictions inherent in the structural tensions of the public realm of appearances. In exploring this last thought, this study shows some comparison with the thought of Rousseau, who gives a fuller and more developed account of these contradictions than does Montaigne. In drawing out Montaigne's appreciation of the ritualistic aspects of life and of actions done for their own sake in the present moment, this study draws comparisons with the more developed and consistently presented views on the same subject of the twentieth-century English philosopher, Michael Oakeshott.

Montaigne's choice and cultivation of the essay form of writing (of which he is one of the creators) is reflective of the skeptical tenor of his thought and writing. His thought is often tentative and exploratory, though it is certainly more than simply the depiction of successive or serial states of consciousness. Following the convention of his time and exploiting the advantages of his agility in Latin and the resources of his personal library, themes are often spun around passages from ancient authors, such as Pyrrho, Plutarch, Seneca, and Horace, among others. The theme of an essay is often not apparent, especially judging from the title, and there are many apparent digressions. It is not always clear what his purposes are, though as this study tries to show, there are discernible and recurring themes and patterns throughout all three books of the *Essais*. And although Montaigne is important, historically speaking, in the sixteenth-century revival of ancient Pyrrhonian and skeptical arguments, it is clear that he uses their tropes and techniques for his own purposes (including, arguably, a defense of the truths of religious revelation), and not simply to induce a suspension of the reader's judgment on all questions he considers.

For this reason, this exposition of Montaigne's views in the *Essais* relies heavily on quotation from individual essays and provides textual context for the quotations as well, in order to get at Montaigne's meaning. In most cases, secondary commentary and critique are relegated to the bibliographic essay and notes. For readers primarily concerned with issues of scholarly controversy or interested in making judgments on issues of scholarly controversy as they read the *Essais,* the bibliographic essay might be the best starting point. For readers who already feel akin to the idea of seeking delight in the present moment (where appropriate) and who are interested in reading Montaigne to make him their own, this latter advice is not intended.

Readers with some French who wish to read the *Essais* in French alongside the English will find them surprisingly straightforward, both syntactically and conceptually, especially in comparison with the more elaborate eighteenth-century style of a writer such as Jean-Jacques Rousseau (though getting used to the archaic Renaissance spelling, e.g. "moy" for "moi," takes a moment). The French editions usually cross-referenced in Montaignian English-language secondary literature are the one-volume Pleiade edition[8] (which also includes Montaigne's travel journals and other materials) and the three-volume Villey edition[9] (which has an interesting appendix with collected reactions to the *Essais* over the centuries). I have used the Villey edition for the French text of the *Essais* in this book.

With regard to the question of Montaigne's *Essais* as a choice for inclusion in a series on great works of Western civilization, several observations may be made. If "Western civilization" is taken in an historical way to be simply the evolved synthesis of the Greek, Roman, Hebraic, and Christian inheritances of the countries of Western Europe and the civilizations elsewhere that they spawned, then Montaigne's *Essais* are clearly an important work. They are part of a Renaissance humanist-intellectual tradition that generated a revived interest in Greco-Roman writers and tried to smooth out the differences between those writers (with more and less success) and their inherited religious traditions or to use them to modify their religious inheritances. And, as we've noted, for the long essay "Apology for Raymond Sebond" alone, Montaigne has been seen as an important figure in the sixteenth-century revival of classical Skeptic arguments that animated (in one direction or another) subsequent Western thinkers such as Descartes, Hume, and Kant.

Yet if Western civilization is taken in a more philosophic sense to indicate a distinctive general orientation toward human life and its relation to the divine and to the world, then Montaigne is arguably an even more important figure, for he takes an important logical potential in the Western synthesis and concretizes it in detail in the *Essais*. Let us unpack this idea.

Arguably, the Western synthesis of Greek rationalism, Roman pragmatism, and Judeo-Christian revelation has produced an orientation toward the individual and toward the individual event in history, which is distinctive. Arguably, this orientation is impelled to take the unique individual and the unique event in history as valuable in themselves and to cherish and cultivate that uniqueness, while at the same time hold that unique person or event in time in view against the backdrop of eternity, or something that transcends time and local mischief. Metaphorically speaking, the complex Western impulse is to stand *both within and without* the stream of time and flux. This outlook is first clearly discernible in the trinitarian reflections of St. Augustine on human beings as unities of body and soul, traveling on a pilgrimage through a secular time-stream devoid of meaning without the insight ignited by the conferral of God's grace.

At first glance, Montaigne might seem like an unlikely candidate for inclusion within this civilizational paradigm. He is wary of human appeals to transcendental grounds in their practical activities, implying that this orientation may lead to arrogance, cruelty, and what we would call ideological fanaticism. He often tries to remind human beings of how much they share with the lower animals (rather than with the divine) as a way of recalling them to their littleness, in the interest of moral and social balance. And he cultivates his own individuality just because it is his, not because it is a reflection of some quality transcending his human nature. Yet this same Montaigne also (in a mixture of Greek and Christian theological conceptions) describes a neo-Platonic, timeless, unchanging, distant God, who without changing bestows his grace on human beings, beings who without that grace can never rise above the contradictions and obstacles of earthly life.[10] The cultivation of his individuality for its own sake (a logical possibility entailed in the very idea of created beings whose existence is a part of their essence[11]), against the backdrop of an unchanging, timeless God, puts Montaigne squarely within this orientation as one who began to develop—in mundane, phenomenological terms—the unique, contingent pole of the Western existential tension, a tendency Tocqueville subsequently associated with democratic cultures. And on the general subject of Montaigne and Western civilization, we may also espy in the *Essais* an orientation within that civilization that rejects in advance (as futile from the standpoint of human repose) anything like the Cartesian and Baconian project for mastery and domination of physical and human nature.

CHAPTER II

Montaigne's Philosophy of Appropriate Living

Part of the excitement and challenge of reading and writing about Montaigne's *Essais* (a testimonial to the vast diversity and contingency of the world) is the impulse these activities engender to make interesting and sustainable generalizations about them. Montaigne himself was caught up in the same kind of enterprise, as have been countless commentators (as well as anonymous readers in many lands). Let us be no exception—let us see what sustainable generalizations can be made about the teachings of the *Essais*.

In my view, Montaigne has a fairly consistent outlook on human contentment or happiness, and a strong case can be made for this theme as the guiding thread through the *Essais*. Before attempting to characterize it, I'll simply observe that Montaigne is not entirely consistent in this outlook in the way a deductive rationalist or a philosophic system builder would be, but he is consistent enough for us to discern a recognizable pattern in his approach to the various activities and compartments of civilized life. And, perhaps, Montaigne's resistance to a thorough theoretical consistency is a part of his teaching about the limits of human reason to manage both its own flux and the flux around it. (Or, alternatively, his thinking, however insightful, may have been a bit muddled, an adjective used by a Spanish ambassador to describe Montaigne as a negotiator.[1])

It can be argued that Montaigne's overriding concern throughout the *Essais* is to find the key to human contentment, or, said differently, to as much psychic harmony as is available to a being immersed in a realm of flux or becoming. In this sense, his aim is similar to that of ancient Greek *eudaimonian* schools of thought (such as those of Plato, Aristotle, the Stoics, Epicureans, and Skeptics), and different from especially Pauline Christianity (or with the later Kantian philosophy) and its emphasis on spiritual goals seen as more important than individual human psychic balance or happiness. (Sin, fear, and repentance are not important themes or concerns of Montaigne, which is one of the reasons the seventeenth-century religious aphorist Blaise Pascal was critical of the *Essais*.) I believe it is uncontroversial that, in Pauline theology, Montaigne would fit the mold of the "psychikos" (one who strives for the contentment of the *psyche*) rather than what St. Paul calls the "spiritual" man.[2]

To discern how to live contently requires, in turn, discerning accurately and realistically one's nature, even if some of that nature involves constant change. Montaigne focuses and experiments on the person he knows best to discern what he is—or the passages or patterns to his "becoming"—as a step on the way to espying the conditional contentment available to a fortunate human being. He discovers certain fairly stable characteristics of himself and, by extension, of some other human beings. As examples, he discovers that although he feels constantly in flux, he has a ruling pattern *(une forme maistresse)* in himself, which desires to communicate and be open toward others; which recognizes the paucity of human reason in grasping the diversity of human experience and the contradictoriness and uncertainty of sense impressions; which enjoys and requires the satisfaction of bodily appetites in moderation; which prefers the delights of private life, especially the cultivation of friendships, over public and political life; which relies heavily on the social, political, and religious customs and traditions he was formed and raised in, owing to the weaknesses of reason to choose better alternatives, and follows them except where they strongly conflict with his ruling pattern; which is averse to cruelty and torture toward others, especially for what we would call "ideological" reasons; and so on. In brief, Montaigne discovers, through self-exploration, a changing self with some abiding features, such as the desire to find a sustainable degree of constancy—a self with limited capacities that requires, for its contentment, recognition of its proper horizons, including religious and political ones. I shall try to show that Montaigne discovers a self that generally restricts itself to activities done for their own sake (rather than as means to other ends); when it cannot avoid engaging in activities employing more instrumental means (such as politics), it engages in them in as "private" a fashion as possible. Too, it uses other human beings as little as possible in purely instrumental ways. The key to human happiness, or at least Montaigne's own happiness, likely comes from recognizing his generic and particular limits, and within the horizons dictated by those limits, trying to participate in activities for their own sake, hence living in the present moment as much as possible—that is, living a life (in philosophic terms) of temporal solipsism whenever realistically possible. Before proceeding, it is instructive to illustrate these Montaignian insights in the *Essais*; to see how they differ from the insights of classical Greek theorists of *eudaimonia* or psychic harmony, such as Aristotle (a frequent target of Montaigne's criticism).

It is characteristic of a teleological thinker such as Aristotle to categorize human activity (not only ethics) in terms of why it is done. Activity or action done for its own sake is highest and most noble for Aristotle, for this is what his self-contained divinity or "unmoved mover" does by simply thinking itself, and human beings become more divine-like in emulating or approximating divine contemplation when possible.[3] They also more fully realize their rational nature as "logos" possessors by engaging in purely theoretical speculation (that is, activity solely for its own sake), and are thereby happier. For Aristotle, the most lowly and necessary activities are those in which thought acts upon matter, that is, in which the activity at hand is done solely for some other sake (for example, making shoes for the sake of wearing them). Middle-range activities are those done partially for their own sake or enjoyment, and partially for some other sake (for example, political activity in which justice is done both for its own sake and also for the sake of preserving the city-state). And, as we have just noted, the highest and happiest human activity is thought thinking or acting upon other thought (not matter), that is, theoretical activity such as philosophy and science. Montaigne shares, by implication with Aristotle, the orientation toward human psychic harmony and the insight that the happiest activities are done for their own sake, but disagrees (to judge by his examples) about which activities can be done for their own sake. As I shall illustrate, for Montaigne, doing something for its own sake is more "subjective" than for Aristotle and has more to do with the state of mind and the intentions in which an individual approaches an activity than with the nature of the subject matter. (Though not always: Public life, for example, is much more difficult to engage in for its own sake than are the actions of private life—one reason Montaigne avoids public life where his conscience will permit.) And the anchor for this view is in the importance, implied by both the drama and content of the *Essais,* of Montaigne's own uniqueness as an individual (and by implication that of others as well). By implication, Montaigne's existence, or his passage in the realm of flux, and his self-conscious appreciation and depiction of the character of this individual existence, is important simply on its own terms, not as the accidental embodiment of a rational essence. Let me try now to illustrate and support the comprehensive view I have attributed to the author of the *Essais* by detailed exploration of relevant passages of his writing and argument.

That Montaigne is most concerned with psychic harmony or balance, rather than with confronting the sinful disorder introduced by the "fall of man" as in the Augustinian and Pauline view, is made clear in the chapter in this study on Montaigne's religious views and is also apparent in his early reliance on Stoic teaching for dealing with the pain of grief. In brief, Montaigne does not share the non-Aristotelian Christian orientation that he is "in" the world but not "of" of the world, for that would imply that life's activities were merely and entirely means or tests for some future purpose. Montaigne, while he is here, is clearly "of" this world, even though he anticipates an afterlife.

On the other hand, he does not immerse himself in this world's pursuit of status and success. Here are some representative observations on this score from two later essays:

> A mon advis c'est le vivre heureusement, non, . . . le mourir heureusement qui faict l'humaine felicité. . . . Si j'avois à revivre, je revivrois comme j'ay vescu. . . .
>
> *In my opinion it is living happily, not . . . dying happily, that constitutes human felicity. . . . If I had to live over again, I would live as I have lived. . . .* [4]
>
> Excusons icy ce que je dy souvent que je me repens rarement et que ma conscience se contente de soy: non comme de la conscience d'un ange ou d'un cheval, mais comme de la conscience d'un homme. . . .
>
> *Let me here excuse what I often say, that I rarely repent and that my conscience is content with itself—not as the conscience of an angel or a horse, but as the conscience of a man. . . .* [5]

On doibt aymer la temperance par elle mesme et pour le respect de Dieu. . . .
On ne peut se vanter de mespriser et combatre la volupté, si on ne la voit, si
on l'ignore, et ses graces, et ses forces, et sa beauté, plus attrayante.

We should love temperance for itself and out of reverence for God. . . . *We
cannot boast of . . . fighting sensual pleasure, if we do not see it or know it,
and its charms, its powers, its alluring beauty.*[6]

. . . puis que ma principale profession en cette vie estoit de la vivre mollement
et plus tost lachement qu'affaireusement, elle m'a osté le besoing de multi-
plier en richesses. . . .

. . . since my principal profession in life was to live comfortably and . . . re-
laxedly . . . it rid me of the need to multiply my riches. . . .[7]

That Montaigne sees his own self as highly mutable and in need of established traditions to keep it from "rolling about" will also be apparent in
our chapters on his political and religious views, and is also an uncontroversial claim. What needs to be established here, and what is especially interesting to a democratic culture like our own (which cultivates the impulses toward self-actualization and self-gratification), is the claim that
Montaigne's general orientation toward living involves the attempt to live
in the present moment, wherever possible, by engaging in activities for
their own sake and enjoyment rather than as steps or means in the accom-
plishment of some external and future purpose or end.

The best way of conveying this Montaignian orientation for the reader is
not to adduce a series of isolated quotations implying this, but to take a
more detailed look at Montaigne's treatment of several themes or activities in which doing things for their own sake (as a state of mind) seem especially appropriate. In this connection, let's look at Montaigne's treatment
of subjects such as friendship, conversation, ritual performance, citizenship, and others.

Take first the activity of conversation, an activity which seems especially suited for present enjoyment, though it is also cultivated widely for
external purposes such as social and political advancement or for information. Let us see how Montaigne treats it in his essay on the art of discussion or conversation *(conferer)*.

In this essay, Montaigne makes clear that he is drawn to argumentative
discourse with others, in person and in small groups, largely for the pleasure it gives him, and not for any social or ostentatious purpose:

J'ayme a contester et à discourir, mais c'est avec peu d'hommes et pour moy. Car de servir de spectable aux grands et faire á l'envy parade de son esprit et de son caquet . . . c'est un mestier tres-messeant. . . .

I love to argue and discuss, but in a small group and for my own sake. For to serve as a spectacle to the great and make a competitive parade of one's wit and chatter is . . . very unbecoming. . . . [8]

Les contradictions donc des jugemens ne m'offencent ny m'alterent; elles m'esveillent seulement et m'exercent. . . . je m'avance vers celuy qui me contredit, qui m'instruit.

So, contradictions of opinions neither offend nor affect me; they merely arouse and exercise me. . . . I go to meet a man who contradicts me, who instructs me. . . . [9]

Et, pourveu qu'on n'y procede d'une troigne trop imperieuse et magistrale, je preste l'espaule aux reprehensions que l'on faict en mes excrits. . . . Mon imagination se contredit elle mesme si souvent et condamne, que ce m'est tout un qu'un autre le face: veu principalement que je ne donne à sa reprehension que l'authorite que je veux.

And provided they do not go about it with too imperious . . . a frown, *I lend a hand to the criticism people make of my writings.* . . . My thinking so often contradicts and condemns itself that it is all one to me if another does the job, *especially seeing that I give his criticism only as much authority as I wish.*[10]

It is clear that for Montaigne the give and take of the conversation is sought for its own sake:

Il me chaut peu de la matiere, et me sont les opinions unes, et la victoire du subject à peu près indifferente. Tout un jour je contesteray paisiblement, si la conduicte du debat se suit avec ordre.

I care little about the subject matter, opinions are all one to me, and *I am almost indifferent about which opinion wins.* I will argue peaceably for a whole day if the debate is conducted with order.[11]

Et tous les jours m'amuse à lire en des autheurs, . . . cherchant leur facon, non leur subject.

And every day I amuse myself reading authors . . . looking for their style, not their subject.[12]

Montaigne even tells us how he conducts discussion and debate not to win so much as for the pleasure of getting the practice of it right: "Just as when I debate with a vigorous man I take pleasure in anticipating his conclusions, . . . [to] save him the trouble of explaining himself, I try to foretell his idea while it is still recent and imperfect. . . ."[13]

Let us look, in further pursuit of his understanding of things done for their own sake, at Montaigne's treatment of friendship in the early essay "Of friendship," devoted to explaining the depth and nature of the extraordinary friendship he had with Étienne de la Boétie. Montaigne employs this rare friendship with a kindred soul as his model for a selfless friendship, distinguished from what he calls "common friendships" (which can even include one's relations with one's doctor and lawyer). Montaigne's understanding of the rare kind of friendship makes it clear that it is entirely for its own sake, devoid of any instrumental advantage whatsoever. He goes to some length to illustrate how genuine friendship differs from instrumental relationships, such as natural, social, hospitable, and erotic ones.

> Car, en general, toutes celles que la volupté ou le profit, le besoin publique ou privé forge et nourrit, en sont d'autant moins belles et genereuses, . . . qu'elles meslent autre cause et but et fruit en l'amitié, qu'elle mesme.
>
> For, in general, *all associations that are forged* and nourished *by pleasure and profit,* by public and private needs, *are* the *less beautiful and noble* . . . insofar as they mix into friendships another . . . reward than friendship itself.[14]
>
> Des enfans aux peres, . . . L'amitié se nourrit de communication qui ne peut se trouver entre eux, pour la trop grande disparité.
>
> *From children toward fathers . . .* Friendship feeds on communication, which cannot exist between them because of their *too great inequality.*[15]
>
> Quant aux mariages . . . et marché qui ordinairement se fait à autres fins.
>
> *As for marriage . . . a bargain* ordinarily *for other ends.*[16]
>
> Au demeurant, ce que nous appellons ordinairement amis et amitiez, ce ne sont qu'accoinctances et familiaritez nouées par quelque occasion ou commodité. . . .
>
> *For the rest,* what we ordinarily call friends and friendships are *nothing but acquaintanceships* and familiarities *found by some chance or convenience.* . . .[17]

The kind of rare friendship Montaigne is describing is so consumed by the enjoyment of a unique self and so much in the present moment, so selfless, so unified, and so non-instrumental as to border on a kind of mystical union reminiscent of the ideals of eighteenth- and nineteenth-century Romanticism:

> En ce noble commerce, les offices et les bienfaits, nourrissiers des autres amitiez, ne meritent pas seulement d'estre mis en compte: cette confusion si pleine de nos volontez en est cause.
>
> *In this noble relationship, service and benefits,* on which other friendships feed, *do not even deserve to be taken into account:* the reason for this is the complete fusion of our wills. . . . [18]
>
> Tout estant par effect commun entre eux, volontez, pensemens, jugemens, biens . . . n'estant qu'un' ame en deux corps. . . .
>
> Everything actually being in common between them—wills, thought, judgments, goods . . . *then relationship being that of one soul in two bodies.* . . . [19]

Nor is there room in such a friendship for "third parties":

> Car cette parfaicte amitié, dequoy je parle, est indivisible: chacun se donne si entier à son amy, qu'il ne luy reste rien a departir ailleurs. . . .
>
> For this perfect friendship I speak of is indivisible: *each one* gives himself so wholly to his friend that *he has nothing left to distribute elsewhere.* . . . [20]

I believe Montaigne's treatment of friendship and conversation makes it unambiguous that he cultivates them for their own sake, for the enjoyment of each moment in itself, without regard for future benefits. But I want to suggest that this was also Montaigne's general orientation toward living, and that it can explain some contradictory emphases in the essays, without recourse to the claim that Montaigne was constantly employing Skeptic techniques for juxtaposing contraries to induce suspension of judgment in himself and the reader. In my view, the very appeal of such Skeptic techniques for Montaigne may have resided in the fact that they provided him with a reasoned justification for taking each moment of time on its own terms insofar as possible, and for savoring the mercurial nature of his own individual personality, rather than having to restrain it. By way of making a case for this view of Montaigne, let us look at a series of assertions from different essays that may at first appear to have no common thread.

... mon entendement ne va pas tousjours avant, il va à reculons aussi. Je ne me deffie guiere moins de mes fantasies pour estre secondes ou tierces que premieres, ou presentes que passées. . . . Moy à cette heure et moy tantost sommes bien deux; mais quand meilleur, je n'en puis rien dire.

... my understanding does not always go forward, it goes backward too. I distrust my thoughts hardly less for being second or third than for being first, or for being present than for being past. . . . *Myself now and myself a while ago are indeed two; but when better, I simply cannot say.*[21]

En mes escris mesmes je ne retrouve pas tousjours l'air de ma premiere imagination: je ne scay ce que j'ay voulu dire . . . Je ne fay qu'aller et venir. . . .

Even in my own writings I do not always find again the sense of my first thought; I do not know what I meant to say. . . . I do nothing but come and go.[22]

Les escrits des anciens, je dis les bons escrits, pleins et solides, me tentent et remuent quasi ou ils veulent; celuy que j'oy me semble tousjours le plus roide; je les trouve avoir raison chacun a son tour, quoy qu'ils se contrarient.

The writings of the ancients . . . the good writings, full and solid, tempt me and move me wherever they please; *the one I am listening to always seems to me the strongest. I find each one right in his turn, although they contradict each other.*[23]

Nous sommes tous de lopins, et d'une contexture si informe et diverse, que chaque piece, chaque momant, faict son jeu.

We are all patchwork, and so shapeless and diverse in composition *that each bit, each moment, plays its own game.*[24]

Je ne peints pas l'estre. Je peints le passage . . . de jour en jour, de minute en minute. Il faut accommoder mon histoire à l'heure. . . . C'est un contrerolle de divers et muables accidens et . . . quand il y eschet, contraires. . . .

I do not portray being: *I portray passing* . . . from day to day, *from minute to minute*. My history needs to be adapted to the moment. . . . This is a record of various and changeable occurrences, and . . . when it so befalls, contradictory ideas. . . . [25]

Tant y a que je me contredits bien à l'adventure, mais la verité . . . Je ne la contredy point. Si mon ame pouvoit prendre pied, je ne m'essaierois pas, je me rousoudrois: elle est tousjours en apprentissage et en espreuve.

So, all in all, I may indeed contradict myself now and then; but in truth . . . I do not contradict. *If my mind would gain a firm foothold, I would not make essays, I would make decisions, but it is always* in *apprenticeship* and *on trial.*[26]

These various assertions or "trial judgments" indicate that for Montaigne the self (his own and that of all but a few rare individuals) is in such flux that its repose is to be sought in giving itself to the moment insofar as this is possible, and ordering a life in which this is intelligently possible most of the time, for example, avoiding a life full of instrumental requirements. In addition, by implication, the essay form of writing, with its provisional judgments and self-experiments would seem the best form or medium for mirroring and grasping, insofar as possible, the structure of human reality (for *almost* all souls). Nevertheless, Montaigne clearly recognizes that some constancy is both necessary and desirable, both for individual identity and repose, and for the possibility of generalization about states of mind and communication with others:

> Or de la cognoissance de cette mienne volubilité j'ay par accident engrendré en moy quelque constance d'opinions, et n'ay guiere alteré les miennes premieres et naturelles. . . . je ne change pas aisément, de peur que j'ay de perdre au change.
>
> *Now from the knowledge of this mobility of mine, I have accidentally engendered in myself a certain constancy of opinions, and have scarcely altered my original natural ones . . . I do not change easily, for fear of losing in the change.*[27]
>
> La vertu ne veut estre suyvie que pour elle mesme. . . . Voyla pourquoy, pour juger d'un homme, il faut suivre longuement et curieusement sa trace; si la constance ne s'y maintient de son seul fondement, . . . laissez le coure: celuy la s'en va avau le vent. . . .
>
> Virtue will not be followed except for her own sake. . . . *That is why, to judge a man, we must follow his traces long and carefully. If he does not maintain consistency for its own sake . . . if changing circumstances make him change his . . . path. . . . Let him go:* that man goes before the wind. . . .[28]

Again, it appears that Montaigne is not simply engaging in the Skeptic technique of equipollent opposition to induce suspension of judgment, but inspecting himself from moment to moment in order to make tentative and qualified judgments about himself. He finds in the variety of his states of mind across time certain recurring patterns in ideas, impulses, appetites, which make up his *character*, that is, an identity constituted by a fairly consistent way of meeting change. For example, he finds a self which seeks repose or contentment over glory; which is content to live in the moment whenever possible; which structures its life in such a way as to be able to do so; which respects the customs, traditions, and rituals it was born to; which is made to communicate with itself and others; which abhors cruelty and torture, and so on.

At this point, let us look at Montaigne's expressed preference for the private realm and the possibilities cultivation of it presents, recalling that at the age of thirty-eight, Montaigne first attempted to retire to his study for a life of self-reflection and self-exploration. A good way to approach this preference is to explore the arguments of two later essays, "Of the useful and the honorable" and "Of three kinds of association"; in the first Montaigne gives his understanding of the requirements of high public life and explains why he prefers to avoid it or do it in as "private" a manner as possible; in the second he explains his taste for three kinds of private association. The burden of the following analysis is to show that private life affords much greater latitude to perform actions for their own sake, and to enjoy people and things for their own sake, in lieu of employing them primarily as means in the achievement of future ends and purposes.

In "Of the useful and the honorable" (a salient theme of the Greco-Roman rhetorical tradition), Montaigne spends some time showing that high political leadership on occasion requires dishonorable, even treacherous, action for the good and preservation of the body politic, and for that reason he is not cut out for it:

> . . . les vices . . . comme les venins à la conservation de nostre santé. S'ils deviennent excusables, d'autant qu'ils nous font besoing et que la necessité commune efface leur vrayre qualité, il faut laisser jouer cette partie aux citoyens plus vigoureux et moins craintifs qui sacrifient leur honneur et leur conscience . . . pour le salut de leur pays; nous autres, plus foibles, prenons des rolles et plus aisez et moins hazardeux.

> *Vices . . . are as poisons for the preservation of our health. If they become excusable, inasmuch as we need them* and the common necessity effaces their true quality, *we still must let this part be played by the more vigorous and less fearful citizens, who sacrifice their honor* and their conscience . . . *for the good of their country.* We who are weaker, let us take parts that are both easier and less hazardous.[29]

Montaigne then goes on to criticize neutrality or fence-sitting during a civil war, but describes in nuanced ways how he has performed his public duties (as negotiator for princes and as mayor) in the most private way possible. In brief, he supports what he considers the just cause but "with moderation and without feverishness" ("I will follow the good side right to the fire, but not into it if I can help it"); is open and "amateurish" in his negotiations, letting others know immediately where he stands ("would rather fail in my mission than fail to be true to myself"); and avoids deception, secrecy, and indebtedness to any prince or power.[30] In brief, he tries to perform his public functions *as nearly as possible as private actions* done for their own sake, and, by good fortune, has been largely successful at it through his openness and evident lack of political ambition:

> Je ne pretens autre fruict en agissant, que d'agir, et n'y attache longues suittes et propositions: chasque action fait particulierement son jeu: porte s'il peut.
>
> *I aspire to no other fruit in acting than to act,* and do not attach to it long consequences and purposes. Each action plays its game individually: *let it strike home if it can.*[31]

That is, Montaigne appears to say that he is prepared to have a limited political or practical effect, if he can do so without immersing himself in the complicated realm of instrumental manipulation of others and events.

Montaigne's approach to private associations and activities is different—here there is the possibility to take people and things on their own terms and to drop the public masks worn in public roles (though many people do not, even in private). Montaigne appears to believe that almost all public lives involve role playing and masking (the Roman republican Cato being an exception), and that individual happiness and repose are not available in this posture toward others. Montaigne distinguishes his three favorite private occupations from "those that I owe the world out of civic duty." The three he discusses are "association" and conversation with talented gentlemen, "association" with the opposite sex, and, the most reliable "association," that with books. His point about each of these intimate associations is that they are done for their own sake and present enjoyment, and do not involve (for him, at any rate) wearing a public mask. Look first at his characterization of the society he seeks with "talented gentlemen":

> La fin de ce commerce, c'est simplement la privauté, frequentation et conference: l'exercice des ames, sans autre fruict.

> *The object of this association is* simply intimacy, fellowship and conversation: *exercise of minds, without any other fruit.*[32]

> S'il plaist à la doctrine de se mesler à nos devis, elle n'en sera point refusée: non magistrale . . . comme de coustume, mais suffragante et docile elle mesme. Nous n'y cherchons qu'à passer le temps; à l'heure d'estre instruicts . . . nous l'irons trouver en son throsne.

> *If learning is to enter our conversation,* she will not be turned out; she will not be magisterial . . . as she usually is, but *subordinate and docile. We seek only to pass the time;* when it is time to be instructed . . . we will go and find her on her throne.[33]

On relating with the opposite sex, Montaigne's point is to avoid a "furious and reckless passion," but also not to play a role like an actor ("though fortune may unjustly reward a passionate mask"), but to put one's own feelings into it:

> . . . de s'y mesler sans amour et sans obligation de volonté, en forme de comediens, pour jouer un rolle commun de l'aage . . . et n'y mettre du sien que les parolles, c'est de vray pourvoyer à sa seureté, mais bien láchement . . . car il est certain que, d'une telle pratique, ceux qui la dressent n'en peuvent esperer aucun fruict qui touche ou satisface une belle ame.

> *. . . to go into it without love and* without binding our will, *like actors, to play the standard role of our . . . customs* and put into it nothing of our own but the words, that is indeed providing for our safety, but in a *cowardly fashion . . .* For it is certain that from *such a relationship* those who form it *can hope for no fruit that will please or satisfy a noble soul.*[34]

Montaigne views books as the most trustworthy and "best provision I have found for this human journey," for he can always count on them to be there when needs them. They are a source of pleasure and pastime, less so a source of utility (for rational exercise in pursuit of the answer to a problem is still instrumental activity):

> J'estudiay, jeune, pour l'ostentation' depuis, un peu, pour m'assagir; a cette heure, pour m'esbatre; jamais pour le quest.

> In my youth *I studied* for ostentation; later, a little to gain wisdom; now, for recreation; never for gain.[35]

> Si quelqu'un me dict que c'est avillir les muses de s'en servir seulement de jouet et de passe-temps, il ne sçait pas, comme moy, combien vaut le plaisir,

le jeu et le passetemps. A peine que je ne die toute autre fin estre ridicule. Je vis du jour a la journée . . . mes desseins se terminent la.

If anyone tells me that it is degrading the Muses to use them only as a plaything and a pastime, he does not know, as I do, the value of pleasure, play and pastime. I would almost say that any other aim is ridiculous. I live from day to day . . . my purposes go no further.[36]

We can see clearly in these last confessions Montaigne's preference for private occupations for the latitude they present to indulge in moods of "temporal solipsism," enjoyment of the present moment for its own sake as the key to repose and contentment. And part of the reason (later developed at great length by Rousseau) for avoiding public life and the realm of instrumental means and mask-wearing is that one is never one's own person:

L'ambition paye bien ses gens de les tenir tousjours en montre, comme la statue d'un marché: «*Magna servitus est magna fortuna.*» Ils n'ont pas seulement leur retraice pour retraitte.

Ambition pays its servants well by keeping them ever on display, like a statue in a market place. Great fortune is great slavery (Seneca). Even their privy is not private.[37]

Another reason for Montaigne's cultivation of the private realm is his love of solitude, an optimal condition for self-reflection devoid of any external or instrumental goal. Montaigne's views on this score are set out in the early essay "Of solitude":

Or, puis que nous entreprenons . . . de nous passer de compagnie, faisons que nostre contentement despende de nous; desprenons nous de toutes les liaisons qui nous attachent à autruy. . . .

Now since we are undertaking to . . . do without company, *let us make our contentment depend on ourselves; let us cut loose all the ties that bind us to others.* . . . [38]

Il se faut reserver une arriereboutique toute nostre, toute franche, en laquelle nous establissons nostre vraye liberté et principale retraicte et solitude.

We must reserve a back shop all our own, entirely free, in which to establish our real liberty and our principal retreat and solitude.[39]

Nous avons une ame contournable en soy mesme; elle se peut faire compagnie;

We have a soul that can be turned back upon itself; it can keep itself company.... [40]

Montaigne is also critical of those who retreat from the public business, only to reproduce it by focusing entirely upon estate management, or by fortifying themselves for another public foray:

> Or la fin, ce crois-je, en est tout' une, d'en vivre plus à loisir et à son aise. Mais on n'en cherche pas tousjours bien le chemin. Souvent on pense avoir quitté les affaires, on ne les a que changez.
>
> *Now the aim of all solitude* ... *is the same: to live more at leisure* and at one's ease. *But people* do not always look for the right way. *Often they think they have left business, and they have only changed it.*[41]

The only apparently instrumental use of solitude that Montaigne condones is in religious lives that eschew the world of power and sensuality to fill "their hearts with the certainty of divine promises for the other life":

> Cette seule fin d'une autre vie heureusement immortelle, merite loyalement que nous abandonnons les commoditez et douceurs de cette vie nostre.
>
> Only this goal of another happily immortal life rightly deserves that we abandon the comforts and pleasures of this life of ours.[42]

Yet before he leaves this subject, Montaigne shears it of its instrumentality as a means to another life by suggesting that for those rare souls capable of a sustained and pure living faith and hope, they achieve a present contentment unequaled:

> ... qui peut embraser son ame de l'ardeur de cette vive foy et esperance, reellement et constamment, il se bastit en la solitude une vie ... delicate au delà de toute autre forme de vie.
>
> And he who can really and constantly kindle his soul with the flame of that living faith ... *builds himself in solitude a life* ... *delightful beyond any other kind of life.*[43]

Before proceeding with further development and illustration of Montaigne's art of living, let us pause to gather up what we have collected thus far. We have seen in the preceding excerpts from the *Essais* a clear preference for actions done for their own sake and for present enjoyment, hence, a preference for private activity, and association, even solitude, and an aversion to the public realm of masks and instrumental means, though not such a strong aversion as to abrogate one's civic obligations and duties to others. And we have seen Montaigne's clear intent to perform public duties in as "private" a manner as possible, even at the expense of failure of a mission if it means being untrue to himself, or to the "ruling patterns" within him. Let us take this encapsulated account of Montaigne's general approach to living and see if we can find support for it throughout the *Essais,* not simply in the ones more obviously germane to this theme. To recast this theme in different terms, in my view, requires an appreciation of the ritualistic aspects of life, including customs and practices not normally thought of as rituals.

Rituals and other activities engaged in ritualistically afford opportunities for performing actions for their own sake, with no external and/or future purpose. Even activities which accomplish a substantive purpose can be performed in a ritualistic state of mind, and thereby avoid some of the alienation of the "means-ends" problem. To take a mundane illustration, there was a time when a gentleman lit a lady's cigarette not because she could not do it for herself but because it was "the practice"; the action was undertaken for its own sake, just to get the practice right (even though a substantive outcome was also achieved). The satisfaction involved in getting the practice correct is "temporally solipsistic," that is, for a brief instant it is isolated from all future and instrumental concerns, even though it may also serve as a means to some future end (such as getting the cigarette lit). Let us look now at other various essays to discern Montaigne's attitude toward any sort of activity performed in a ritualistic state of mind, however implicitly so, or, said differently, activities engaged in for present enjoyment rather than primarily as means instrumental to a future end.

In the early essays of the first volume we see several recurring themes which contribute to this outlook, such as mastery of fear of death in order even to be capable of present enjoyment, and Montaigne's personal aversion to lying and manipulation owing to a bad memory and, hence, inability to maintain a successful pattern of lying and deceit. Yet besides the essays on friendship and on solitude (which we have already considered), another extended treatment of the alienation of means-ends activity occurs in the (unlikely) essay, "Of the inequality that is between us."[44] This essay develops into a variation on a theme of the Roman lyrical poet Horace about the unhappiness of high public life when compared to a private life of repose and contentment, and also draws heavily on the complaints (about his life) of the tyrant Hiero in Xenophon's famous dialogue of the same name. (Montaigne does not take up the possibility that Xenophon has Hiero exaggerate the trials and tribulations of the tyrannical life in order to discourage others from wanting to displace him.) Let us look at Montaigne's construction of this theme, which has several steps.

Montaigne begins by observing that when we judge animals such as horses and greyhounds, we judge them by such qualities as vigor and speed, respectively, but that our tendency when judging other human beings is to judge by all that surrounds them: "a great retinue, a beautiful palace, so much influence, so much income." He then asks, "Why do we not likewise judge a man by what is his own?" And, "Why in judging a man do you judge him all wrapped up in a package?"[45] The obvious answer to this question, which Montaigne does not make explicit, is that these "trappings" are symbols or representations of a person's influence and power over others, and this is what most people are interested in. Montaigne simply moves on to suggest that those with much power and influence live completely public lives and have little repose and contentment. Instead of judging by external relations, we should endeavor to see if "his soul is composed, equable, and content . . . and by this judge the extreme differences that are between us." Even the external goods of fortune "still need taste to enjoy them. It is the enjoying not the possessing, that makes us happy."[46]

Montaigne then goes into a brief analysis of why ruling others is such an unpleasant life. Ruling is a difficult thing, which gives the mind no rest:

> Certes, ce n'est pas peu de chose que d'avoir à regler autruy, puis qu'à regler nous mesmes il se presente tant de difficultez. Quant au commander, qui semble estre si doux, considerant l'imbecillité du jugement humain et la difficulté du chois és choses nouvelles et doubteuses, je suis fort de cet advis, qu'il est bien plus aisé et plus plaisant de suivre que de guider, et que c'est un grand sejour d'esprit de n'avoir a tenir qu'une voie tracée et à respondre que de soy. . . .

> Truly it is no small thing to have to rule others, since in ruling ourselves so many difficulties occur. As for commanding, which seems to be so sweet: considering the imbecility of human judgment and the difficulty of choice in new and doubtful things, *I am of the opinion that it is much easier and pleasanter to follow than to guide, and that it a great rest for the mind to have only to hold to a mapped-out path and to be answerable only for oneself.* . . .[47]

In order to add weight to these claims, Montaigne cites some of the classic complaints of the life of tyrants and powerful public persons—lack of privacy, lack of sincerity in the utterances and actions of others, constant vigilance, and so on. And he also indicates the slavery in a life of ambition centered around obtaining the favors of the powerful:

> La subjection essentielle et effectuelle ne regarde d'entre nous que ceux qui s'y convient et qui ayment à s'honnorer et enrichir par tel service: car qui se veut tapir en son foyer . . . il est aussi libre que le Duc de Venise.

> The real and essential subjection is only for those among us who go seeking it and who like to gain honors and riches by such service; *for anyone who wants to ensconce himself by his hearth . . . is as free as the Doge of Venice.*[48]

Montaigne concludes this essay by observing that the real advantages of princes are shared by persons of moderate fortune, and he cites an anecdote about a conversation between the Greek king Pyrrhus and his wise counselor Cyneus on the eve of the invasion of Italy, a conversation which explicitly illustrates the alienation in pursuing means for instrumental ends. Cyneus asks Pyrrhus why he is invading Italy and learns through a series of questions and answers that Pyrrhus's goal is to be master of Italy, then Greece and Spain, and finally Africa, in order to rest content and be at ease. Cyneus then responds:

> Pour Dieu, Sire, rechargea lors Cyneas, dictes moy à quoy il tient que vous ne soyez dés à présent, si vous voulez, en cet estat? pourquoy ne vous logez vous, des cette heure, où vous dictes aspirer, et vous espargnez tant de travail et de hazard que vous jettez entre deux?

> "In God's name, Sire . . . tell me what keeps you from being in that condition right now. . . . Why don't you settle down this very moment in that state you say you aspire to, and spare yourself all the intervening toil and risks?"[49]

Other themes in the first book of essays that support our characterization of Montaigne's fairly consistent outlook include his disparagement of human reason and judgment for its uncertainty and confusion (hence, by implication, the futility of complicated instrumental plans), and his recurring observations about the natural and vast diversity of human customs and human selves which resist, by implication, the imposition of instrumental plans, and demand, in the order of things, to be taken on their own terms. There is also an essay ("Of vain subtleties") which describes a commonality between a primitive ignorance before knowledge and a learned ignorance which comes after knowledge for a few wise individuals who recapture through reflection the ability to take things on their own terms:

> La bestise et la sagesse se rencontrent en mesme point de sentiment et de resolution à la souffrance des accidens humains: les Sages gourmandent et commandent le mal, et les autres l'ignorent. . . .
>
> *Stupidity and wisdom meet at the same point of feeling and resolving to endure human accidents.* The wise curb and control the evil; the others are not aware of it.[50]

The only theme in the first book which *appears* to contradict our characterization of living in the present moment, insofar as possible, occurs in the essay "That our happiness must not be judged until after our death." Montaigne's point in this two-page essay is the rather stoic one that happiness in this life depends on the tranquility and assurance of a well-ordered soul, but that we can not be sure, until someone meets death and the public mask is torn away, whether the life in question was truly in repose or only a pose or sham:

> Mais à ce dernier rolle de la mort et de nous, il n'y a plus que faindre. . . . Voylà pourquoy se doivent à ce dernier traict toucher et esprouver toutes les autres actions de nostre vie. . . . Je remets à la mort l'essay du fruict de mes estudes. Nous verrons là si mes discours me partent de la bouche, ou du cœur.
>
> But in the last scene, between death and ourselves, there is no more pretending. . . . That is why all the other actions of our life must be tried and tested by this last act. . . . *I leave it to my death to test the fruit of my studies. We shall see them whether my reasonings come from my mouth or from my heart.*[51]

If Montaigne means to say here that he himself must await the moment of death to know if he has been in repose in trying to live in the present moment or was only maintaining a pose, then these sentiments would present a problem for our characterization of his general orientation toward living. Yet, if he is simply saying (which seems more likely) that other people may, at his death, judge the sincerity and accuracy of the self-portrait he has given in the *Essais,* and that he may merely be confirmed, when he meets death (for everyone may have self-doubts), in the life he had practiced, then these sentiments do not require us to modify our characterization. For as Montaigne makes explicit in the subsequent essay ("That to philosophize is to learn to die"), *present* rest and repose of the soul requires overcoming the fear of death:

> Car, comme il est impossible qu'elle se mette en repos, pendant qu'elle le craint: si elle s'en asseure aussi, elle se peut venter, qui est chose comme surpassant l'humaine condition....
>
> *For it is impossible for the soul to be at rest while she fears death,* so, if she can gain assurance against it, she can boast of things beyond man's estate....[52]

It would appear, then, that in the case of sophisticated or learned ignorance, knowledge must be used instrumentally to overcome the fear of death as a step or stage in the capacity (when and where appropriate) to live noninstrumentally in the present moment, and to perform public, instrumental duties in as "private" a manner as possible, even at the risk of failure.

In the second book of essays, support for our characterization of Montaigne's general approach to living can be found first in a digression within an essay on the affection of fathers for their children, where Montaigne explains that he avoids the world of complicated means and strategies because he isn't very good at it and prefers to escape from it in distraction:

> Si les autres me pippent, au moins ne me pippe je pas moy mesmes à m'estimer capable de m'en garder, ny à me ronger la cervelle pour m'en rendre. Je me sauve de telles trahisons en mon propre giron, non par une inquiete ... curiosite, mais par diversion plustost et resolution.
>
> If others deceive me, at least *I do not deceive myself,* either *by thinking myself capable of guarding against their deception,* or by racking my brains to make myself capable. *I escape* from such betrayals in my own bosom, not by a restless ... curiosity, but *rather by diversion* and resolution.[53]

And in an essay on books (written years before the treatment of books in the essay on three kinds of association), Montaigne gives insight into two different ways of living in the present moment, of enjoying something for its own sake. In this eleven-page essay, Montaigne makes it clear that he does not possess knowledge of anything, except perhaps himself, and that his various opinions on various learned authors are meant subjectively "to declare the measure of my sight, not the measure of things."[54] He explains his intermittent reading habits, directed for the most part toward present pleasure and amusement, not tortuously obtained knowledge of the world:

> Je souhaiterois bien avoir plus parfaicte intelligence des choses, mais je ne la veux pas achepter si cher qu'elle couste.... Il n'est rien pourquoy je me vueille rompre la teste, non pas pour la science, de quelque grand pris qu'elle soit.... Si ce livre me fasche, j'en prens un autre; et ne m'y addonne qu'aux heures où l'ennuy de rien faire commence à me saisir.

> I should certainly like to have a more perfect knowledge of things, but I do not want to buy it as dear as it costs.... *There is nothing for which I want to rack my brains, not even knowledge, however great its value....* If this book wearies me, I take up another; and *I apply myself to it only at the moments when the boredom of doing nothing begins to grip me.*[55]

But then Montaigne concedes (at least at this point in his life) that he also does some reading "which mingles a little more profit with the pleasure."[56] Montaigne goes on to explain that there are a few works, especially the epistles of Seneca and the moral essays of Plutarch, which he reads not for the sake of knowledge or eloquence but to become wiser and learn to arrange his ways better. He especially likes the epistles of Seneca because their insights are "in detached pieces that do not demand the obligation of long labor, of which I am incapable."[57] And he informs us that he dislikes authors like Cicero, who spends too much time in scholastic definitions and arrangements: "I want a man to begin with the conclusion.... In general I ask for books that make use of learning, not those that build it up."[58] Yet in both cases (pleasure and "profit") it is clear that Montaigne is living in the present moment in his reading, since even the acquisition of wise insights, which may be used instrumentally in one's life at future times, provide a present enjoyment as they are internalized and become a part of one's character in the very act of understanding.

Montaigne's discussion of virtue in the essay "Of cruelty" gives us insight into forms of living for their own sake which differ from and surpass his own. This discussion also makes clear that actions done for their own sake do not exclude the possibility of conflict and overcoming of opposition (as a step in the achievement of psychic harmony). Let us look at his reasoning here.

Montaigne begins by distinguishing virtue from mere goodness and innocence in suggesting that, as he uses it, virtue "presupposes difficulty and contrast, and that it cannot be exercised without opposition." He then describes three forms of virtuous life, the last and lowest of which (his own, for example) does not really merit the word virtue and should more properly be called innocence, since by birth and/or upbringing it had for the most part moderate desires which required no great self-overcoming or self-control:

> Ma vertu, c'est une vertu, ou innocence, pour mieux dire, accidentale et fortuite. Si je fusse nay d'une complexion plus déreglée, je crains qu'il fut allé piteusement de mon faict. Car je n'ay essayé guiere de fermeté en mon ame pour soustenir des passions. . . .
>
> My virtue is a virtue, or should I say an innocence, that is accidental and fortuitous. *If I had been born with a more unruly disposition, I fear it would have gone pitifully with me. For I have not experienced much firmness in my soul to withstand passions. . . .*[59]

The two genuine forms of virtue he describes involve overcoming through reason some great passion, and, secondly, a very rare form of virtue in which the soul has so mastered passions, such as fear and lust, that they do not even arise. In this connection, Montaigne discusses the cases of Cato the younger and Socrates. It is in this latter, very rare category of virtue that we see Montaigne's appreciation of virtue done solely for its own sake, continually in the present moment, so to speak.

He begins this discussion by noting the instances of ancient Stoic and especially Epicurean philosophers who begin to test their virtue by using as "playthings" shame, fever, poverty, death and torture, *and eventually achieve a "kind of virtue which has climbed so high that it not only despises pain but rejoices in it. . . ."*[60] He then takes up the case of the younger Cato at the moment of his painful suicide in honor of republican liberty, and speculates that his equanimity and composure were not simply a matter of self-mastery, but that he must have felt bliss in such a noble action, for its own sake, and not as a matter of subsequent reputation or for any practical effect:

> Tesmoing le jeune Caton. Quand je le voy mourir . . . je ne puis croire qu'il se maintint seulement en cette démarche que les regles de la secte Stoique luy ordonnoient. . . . Je croy sans doubte qu'il sentit du plaisir et de la volupté en une si noble action, et qu'il s'y agrea plus qu'en autre de celles de sa vie. . . .
>
> *Witness the younger Cato. When I see him dying . . . I cannot be content to believe that he merely maintained himself in the attitude that the rules of the Stoic sect ordained . . . I believe without a doubt that he felt pleasure and*

bliss in so noble an action, and that he enjoyed himself more in it than in any other action of his life.⁶¹

> ... non pas esguisée par quelque esperance de gloire ... mais pour la beauté de la chose mesme en soy: laquelle il voyoit bien plus à clair et en sa perfection ... que nous ne pouvons faire.

> *This enterprise was not spurred by some hope of glory ... but was undertaken for the beauty of the very thing in itself,* which he ... saw much more clearly in its perfection than we can see it.⁶²

Similarly, in the death of Socrates (though less tragic than Cato's), Montaigne speculates that his composure in the face of death came not merely from a soul free of fear and passion but contained also a joy at the release of earthly fetters:

> Et qui ... peut se conenter d'imaginer Socrates seulement franc de crainte et de passion en l'accident ... de sa condemnation? Et qui ne reconnoit en luy ... je ne sçay quel contentement nouveau et une allegresse enjoüee en ses propos et façons dernieres?

> *And who ... can be satisfied with imagining Socrates as merely free from fear and passion* in the incident of ... his condemnation? And *who does not recognize in him ... I know not what new contentment,* and a blithe cheerfulness in his last words and actions?⁶³

> ... accuse il pas une pareille douceur et joye en son ame, pour estre desenforgée des incommodités passées ... ?

> ... does he not betray a like sweetness and joy in his soul at being unfettered by past discomforts ... ?⁶⁴

Montaigne's analysis of these rare instances of virtue show yet another instance of his appreciation of acts lived entirely in the present moment (even where outside the orbit of Montaigne's capabilities) and his aversion to means-ends instrumentalities. Since such greatness is beyond his capacities, Montaigne prefers to live as much as possible within a private realm of friendship and conversation where he is more capable of action and utterance for its own sake, more capable of participating in the kind of conditional, earthly immortality achieved in consummation of the present moment.

Montaigne's view on reputation in popular opinion in the essay "Of glory" we can deduce in general before reading the essay. Given his approach to living, he cannot possibly praise something done for the instrumental and future purpose of glory in the eyes and memory of others (except insofar as this is intended to deflect their hostility and attention toward one's private life). And this is exactly the argument he makes in this essay.

Difficult as it is for such changeable and "double" beings as ourselves, we should strive to live honorably and virtuously for its own sake, rather than for the mere reputation of our acts to satisfy our vanity:

> Ce n'est pas pour la montre que nostre ame doit jouer son rolle, c'est chez nous, au dedans, où nuls yeux ne donnent que les nostres: . . . . «Non emolumento aliquo, sed ipsius honestatis decore.»
>
> It is not for show that our soul must play its part, it is at home, within us, where no eyes penetrate but our own. . . . *Not for profit, but for the beauty of merit itself.*[65]

The reason for this is that it is unintelligent to base one's repose and tranquillity on so uncertain a goal as esteem in popular opinion (and furthermore, someone will not always be watching during our most important trials). Genuine tranquillity is to be sought in the contentment of the soul in well-doing for its own sake:

> Toute la gloire que je pretens de ma vie, c'est de l'avoir vescue tranquille: . . . selon moy. Puis que la philosophie n'a sçeu trouver aucune voye pour la tranquillité, qui fust bonne en commun, que chacun la cherche en son particulier!
>
> *All the glory that I aspire to in my life is to have lived it tranquilly . . . according to me. Since philosophy has not been able to find a way of tranquillity that is suitable for all, let everyone seek it individually.*[66]

> Moy, je tiens que je ne suis que chez moy; et, de cette autre mienne vie qui loge en la connoissance de mes amis. . . . je sçay bien que je n'en sens . . . ny jouyssance que par la vanité d'une opinion fantastique.
>
> *As for me, I hold that I exist only in myself;* and as for that other life of mine that lies in the knowledge of my friends . . . I know that I feel no . . . enjoyment of it except by the vanity of a fanciful opinion.[67]

In brief, as we expected, Montaigne eschews the pursuit of glory or reputation in the eyes of the public at large for its own sake and follows the (Epicurean) rule of "conceal your life" in order to seek present contentment within himself by living as un-instrumentally as possible. He even suggests that pursuing glory for the instrumental goals or advantages it brings (good will of others, insulation from insult and injury) is preferable from the standpoint of tranquillity to pursuing glory for its own sake. Although this might appear to be an exception to our characterization of Montaigne's art of living (preferring advantages over the thing itself), a moment's analysis will show that it is not an exception. For the pursuit of glory requires action and utterance so dependent on the future reactions of others that, carefully speaking, it is a perversion of language to speak of it for its own sake, and probably the only reason Montaigne employs the phrase, even to reject its suitability, is to quarrel with the ancient philosopher Carneades who had provocatively counseled pursuit of glory for its own sake.[68]

The rather long essay "Of presumption," on the human tendency to form "an over-good opinion" of one's own worth, also supports and illustrates our characterization of Montaigne's art of living in various ways. Montaigne's main point about an inflated sense of self-worth is that it leads to dissatisfaction with what one has (since one feels one deserves more) and a yearning and preoccupation with obtaining more, or what some others have:

> ... je diminue du juste prix les choses que je possede, de ce que je les possede; et hausse le prix aux choses, d'autant qu'elles sont estrangieres, absentes et non miennes. Cette humeur s'espand bien loin ... engendre mespris de ce qu'on tient et regent.

> ... I lower the value of things I possess, because I possess them, and raise the value of things that are foreign, absent and not mine. *This humor spreads very far ... and ... breeds contempt of what we hold and control.*[69]

Needless to say, this dissatisfaction takes one outside oneself and immerses one in an alienating pursuit of instrumental means for future ends. As an illustration of the tyranny of means involved in high ambition, Montaigne cites the case of Machiavelli's advice to princes (considering only the success of their political affairs, not the good of their conscience and of fidelity) and suggests that it might be defensible advice if wicked deeds could be done once and for all in a single instance:

> Mais il n'en va pas ainsi. On rechoit souvent en pareil marché. ... Le gain qui les convie à la premiere desloyauté (et quasi toujours il s'en presente comme à toute autres meschancetez. ...), mais ce premier gain apporte infinis dommages suivants. ...

> *But this is not the way it goes. You often fall into the same sort of bargain again.... The gain that lures them to the first breach of faith—and almost always there is gain in it, as in all other wicked deeds... This first gain brings after it endless losses....*[70]

Montaigne prefers to stay within himself whenever possible, owing to a strong self-love, a bad memory for detail, a strong aversion to deception, a strong love of candor, indecision in thought and action, and the good fortune to have inherited sufficient means to live at leisure:

> Ne pouvant reigler les evenemens, je me reigle moy-mesme, et m'applique à eux, s'ils ne s'appliquent à moy.

> Not being able to rule events, I rule myself, and adapt myself to them if they do not adapt themselves to me.[71]

> J'ay une ame toute sienne, accoustumée à se conduire à sa mode.... je n'ay rien cerché et n'ay aussi rien pris.... Je n'ay eu besoin que de la suffisance de me contenter....

> I have a soul all its own, accustomed to conducting itself in its own way.... *I have sought nothing and also acquired nothing.* ... The only ability I have needed is the ability to content myself with my lot....[72]

In developing this theme of self-devotion, Montaigne uses phrases that support our characterization of his propensity to live in the present moment:

> Tout ce que les autres en distribuent à une infinie multitude d'amis et de connoissans, à leur gloire ... je le rapporte tout au repos de mon esprit et à moy.

> *All the affection that others distribute to an infinite multitude of friends* and acquaintances, to their glory ... *I devote entirely to the repose of my mind and to myself.*[73]

> Le monde regarde tousjours vis à vis; moy, je replie ma veue au dedans, je la plante, je l'amuse la.... je me contrerolle, je me gouste.... moy je me roulle en moy mesme.

> The world always looks straight ahead; as for me, I turn my gaze inward, I fix it there and keep it busy.... *I take stock of myself, I taste myself.... I roll about in myself.*[74]

It would not be an exaggeration to say that in passages such as these, and in the *Essais* generally, Montaigne polishes up and tries to make attractive his own natural penchant for cultivation of the private, the unique, and the idiosyncratic by implying that this approach to living provides the realistic opportunity for the repose and contentment of the vast majority of human beings.

In the essay "Of giving the lie," on the importance of truthfulness and the corruption of dissimulation, Montaigne gives us an explicit statement of the superiority of the pleasures of the private and inward life to those of the public life:

> Les plus delicieux plaisirs, si se digerent-ils au dedans, fuyent à laisser . . . la veue non seulement du peuple, mais d'un autre.
>
> *Indeed, the most delightful pleasures are digested inwardly,* avoid leaving . . . the sight not only of the public but of any other person.[75]
>
> Nature nous a estrenez d'une large faculté à nous entretener à part, et nous y appelle souvent pour nous apprendre que nous nous devons en partie à la société, mais en la meilleure partie à nous.
>
> *Nature* has made us a present of a broad capacity for entertaining ourselves, and often calls us to do so, *to teach us that we owe ourselves in part to society, but in the best part to ourselves.*[76]

Montaigne also makes explicit here that his book, though written for the amusement of others, has primarily been for its own sake, that is, for his own self-discovery and self-formation:

> Me peignant pour autry, je me suis peint en moy de couleurs plus nettes que n'estoyent les miennes premieres. Je n'ay pas plus faict mon livre que mon livre m'a faict, livre consubstantiel à son autheur, d'une occupation propre, membre de ma vie; non d'une occupation et fin tierce et estrangere comme tous autres livres.
>
> Painting myself for others, I have painted my inward self with colors clearer than my original ones. I have no more made *my book* than my book has made me—a book co-substantial with its author—*an integral part of my life, not concerned with some third-hand, extraneous purpose, like . . . other books.*[77]

The brief essay "Of evil means employed to a good end" presents an interesting conundrum, which, when unraveled, supports our characterizations of Montaigne's approach to living. We are surprised in this essay to see Montaigne, usually so outspoken against cruelty and torture of any kind, giving a qualified approbation ("an admirable example") of the Roman gladiatorial games in which

> de voir tous les jours en sa presence cent, deux cens, et mille couples d'hommes . . . se hacher en pieces avecques une si extreme fermeté de courage qu'on ne leur vist lácher une parolle de foiblesse. . . .
>
> every day before their eyes a hundred . . . even a thousand pairs of men . . . hack each other to pieces with such extreme firmness of courage that they were observed never to let slip a word of weakness. . . . [78]

It turns out that Montaigne is able to give the qualified approbation of Roman gladitorial practice (where he cannot for other ancient instances of cruelty) because it was being used to teach the people contempt for the dangers of death, a state of mind we have seen Montaigne previously consider as essential to the capacity to live fully in the present moment:

> car, s'il se faut débaucher, on est plus excusable le faisant pour la santé de l'ame que pour celle du corps: comme les Romains dressoient le peuple à la vaillance et au mespris des dangiers et de la mort par ces furieux spectacles de gladiateurs. . . .
>
> *For if we must go to excess, it is more excusable to do so for the health of the soul than for that of the body; as the Romans trained the people to valor and contempt for dangers and death by those furious spectacles of gladiators.* . . . [79]

Montaigne's views in the essay "Of anger" are not deducible from our characterizations of his art of living, but they are consistent with it. He thinks we should try to master anger as much as possible, for there "is no passion that so shakes the clarity of our judgment as anger."[80] In brief, it is to be avoided because it takes away our self-control and diminishes our ability to order our lives around private pursuits:

> . . . car nous remuons les autres armes, cette cy nous remue; nostre main ne la guide pas, c'est elle qui guide nostre main; elle nous tient, nous ne la tenons pas.
>
> For we move other weapons, this one moves us; our hand does not guide it, it guides our hand; *it holds us, we do not hold it*.[81]

When anger cannot be avoided, Montaigne counsels effort to keep it as brief, to the point, and private as possible; he also endorses feigning it without any real emotion on occasion, for practical purposes such as governing his house.

Montaigne gives us an analysis of the dangers for the soul of high political ambition in the essay "The Story of Spurina" by focusing on the career of Julius Caesar, an otherwise great man who sought "his glory in the ruin of his Country" and the subversion of its great republic. Montaigne illustrates how Caesar's fine qualities (sobriety, eloquence, learning, military genius, discipline, generosity) were "spoiled and stifled by the furious passion of ambition"[82] which drove him to treat all his actions as instrumental to the end of his own glory:

> Somme, ce seul vice, à mon advis, perdit en luy . . . le plus riche naturel qui fut onques, et a rendu sa memoire abominable à tous les gens de bien. . . .

> To sum up, *this single vice . . . ruined in him the finest and richest nature . . . and made his memory abominable to all good men. . . .*[83]

> D'un homme liberal elle en rendit un voleur publique pour fournir à cette profusion et largesse, et luy fit dire ce vilain et tresinjuste mot, que si les plus meschans et perdus hommes du monde luy avoient esté fidelles au service de son agrandissement, il les cheriroit et avanceroit de son pouvoir. . . . l'enyvra d'une vanité si extreme qu'il. . . . osoit se vanter en presence de ses concitoyens d'avoir rendu cette grande Republique Romaine un nom sans forme . . . et dire que ses responces devoient meshuy servir de loix. . . .

> *Of a liberal man, it made a public robber*, to provide for his profusion and largess, and it made him utter that . . . very unjust saying, that if the most wicked . . . had been faithful to him in the service of his aggrandizement, he would cherish and advance them by his power. . . . *It intoxicated him with a vanity so extreme that he dared to boast that he had made the great Roman Republic a name without form . . . and to say that his answers must henceforth serve as laws. . . .*[84]

The story of Caesar's ambition and its effects on him is clearly emblematic for Montaigne of an alienated life which necessarily reduces all other individuals and activities (and even its own virtues) to instrumental means in the pursuit of status in the eyes of others, such that nothing in it can be said to have been done for its own sake. Montaigne seems especially vexed at Caesar for spoiling, through ambition, so many admirable virtues, especially military-related ones that Montaigne explicitly praises in another essay on Caesar's military methods. As for Montaigne's clear admiration for (and fascination with) military virtue, we can only speculate by observing that in addition to the importance for him of valor in the face of death, and of the esteem of his social class,[85] the intense experience of facing death courageously in combat is as clear an instance as humanly possible of living entirely within the present moment, a moment when time seems to stand still:

> Celuy qui meurt en la meslée, les armes à la main, il n'estudie pas lors la mort, il ne la sent ny ne la considere: l'ardeur du combat l'emporte.
>
> The man who dies in the melee, arms in hand, does not then study death; he neither feels it nor considers it; *he is carried away by the heat of the battle.*[86]

We have already looked at several of the essays of Book III ("On conversation," "The useful and the honorable," "Three kinds of association") in our initial characterization of Montaigne's art of living. Now let us look at some others for further illustration and amplification. "Of diversion" is concerned with the ways in which our minds can learn to divert us from intense thoughts of fear and pain, for only the great (such as Socrates) can successfully "meet troubles head on":

> On luy faict peu choquer les maux de droit fil . . . on la luy faict decliner et gauchir. . . . C'est à faire à ceux de la premiere classe de s'arrester purement à la chose, la considerer, la juger.
>
> We rarely make the soul meet troubles head on . . . we have to avoid and sidestep them. . . . *It is only for first-class men to dwell purely on the thing itself, consider it, and judge it.*[87]

Diversion is the remedy for the vast majority of human beings:

> Nous pensons tousjours ailleurs; l'esperance d'une meilleure vie nous arreste et appuye, ou l'esperance de la valeur de nos enfans, ou la gloire future de nostre nom, ou la fuite des maux de cette vie, ou la vengeance. . . .
>
> *Our thoughts are always elsewhere;* the hope of a better life stays and supports us, or the hope of our children's worth, or the future glory of our name, or flight from the ills of this life, or vengeance. . . . [88]

For most people, diversion, even instrumental diversions such as thoughts of glory and ambition, are necessary to fend off paralyzing fear and pain, and happily, Montaigne says, the capacity for such diversion is supported by the inconstancy of general human nature:

> Nature procede ainsi par le benefice de l'inconstance: car le temps, qu'elle nous a donné pour souverain medecin de nos passions, gaigne son effaict . . . par là, que, fournissant autres et autres affaires à nostre imagination. . . .

> Nature proceeds thus by the benefit of our inconstancy. *For time, which she has given us as the sovereign physician of our passions, gains its effect . . . in this way, furnishing our imagination with other and every other business. . . .* [89]

> Peu de chose nous divertit et destourne, car peu de chose nous tient. Nous ne regardons gueres les subjects en gros et seuls; ce sont des circonstances ou des images menues et superficieles qui nous frapent. . . .

> *It takes little to divert us and distract us,* for it takes little to hold us. We scarcely look at things in gross and alone; it is the minute and superficial circumstances and notions that strike us. . . . [90]

Montaigne describes in this context his own techniques of diversion, now using one strong passion (e.g., love) to distract him from another strong one (e.g., grief), now engaging in multiple variations:

> . . . une aigre imagination me tient; je trouve plus court, que de la dompter, la changer; je luy en substitue, si je ne puis une contraire, aumoins un'autre. Tousjours la variation soulage, dissout et dissipe. Si je ne puis la combatre, je luy eschape. . . . je me sauve dans la presse d'autres amusemens. . . .

> *A painful notion takes hold of me; I find it quicker to change it than subdue it. I substitute* a contrary one for it . . . or at all events *a different one*. Variation always solaces, dissolves and dissipates. If I cannot combat it, I escape it. . . . By changing . . . I escape into the throng of other occupations. . . . [91]

Montaigne's analysis of techniques of diversion is consistent with what we have seen already. In the interest of repose, fear and pain must be abated. For almost all human beings (including Montaigne) this requires use of distractions and diversions. Diversions may involve use of instrumental means, but the less instrumental and less alienating diversions may be used to divert from the more so (for instance, Montaigne's diversion of a young prince's mind from vengeance to considerations of reputation and ambition); and some diversions, such as conversation and writing, may be done entirely for their own sake. Montaigne's discussion of escape from painful notions by losing himself in diverse and solacing new occupations is emblematic of the "temporal solipsism" we have described which seeks repose in the delight of the present moment.

In keeping with Montaigne's insistence on openness, much of the long essay "On some verses of Virgil" is a rambling and candid discussion of the sexual and conjugal mores of Montaigne's time and social class, including his own sexual proclivities; but there are also explicit and implicit reflections on what leads to happiness and repose in human beings which are useful for our general characterizations. Montaigne is very explicit that humans beings are mixtures of body and soul (in a "tight brotherly bond"), and that human contentment, especially the "cheerful tranquillity" which Montaigne seeks, requires the continuing satisfaction of bodily appetites (this is one area in which Montaigne is simply silent on Christian morality):

> La philosophie n'estrive point contre les voluptez naturelles, pourveu que la mesure y soit joincte, et en presche la moderation, non la fuite. . . .
>
> *Philosophy does not strive against natural pleasures, provided that measure goes with them; she preaches moderation in them, not flight.*[92]
>
> Pouvons nous pas dire qu'il n'y a rien en nous, pendant cette prison terrestre, purement ny corporel ny spirituel, et que injurieusement nous dessions un homme tout vif. . . .
>
> *May we not say that there is nothing in us during this earthly imprisonment that is purely either corporeal or spiritual, and that we do wrong to tear apart a living man. . . .* [93]
>
> En pareil cas, aux plaisirs corporels, est-ce pas injustice d'en refroidir l'ame, et dire, qu'il l'y faille entrainer comme à quelque obligation. . . . C'est a elle plus tost de les couver et fomenter. . . .
>
> *In a . . . case . . . of bodily pleasures, is it not unjust to cool the soul towards them* and say that she should be dragged to them as to some . . . obligation. . . . *It is rather for her to hatch them and foment them. . . .* [94]

Montaigne even explains in this connection that just as in his youth he sought balance by restraining sensual pleasure, now in older age, when beset by bodily ills, he deliberately lets himself "go a bit to license" in hopes of distracting his soul from its bodily burdens: "I defend myself against temperance as I once did against sensual pleasure."[95] All of this is consistent with Montaigne's "philosophy" of achieving a "pleasant and cheerful tranquillity" and a "gay and sociable wisdom" devoid of harsh and austere behavior, through delight in the present moment of experience: "*My philosophy is in action, in natural and present practice.*"[96] For either extreme denial or extreme satisfaction of bodily appetites, by implication, compels most human beings to live in anticipation of a future condition rather than take pleasure in the present for its own sake.

"Of coaches" has some observations on the European "contagion" of the new worlds of Mexico and Peru, which are relevant to our thesis about Montaigne's eschewal of instrumentality toward things and other people. Montaigne suggests that "we" trampled over the new world because "we" were more advanced in the technology of war and in the practice of treachery toward others:

> Bien crains-je que nous aurons bien fort hasté sa declinaison et sa ruyne par nostre contagion, et que nous luy aurons bien cher vendu nos opinions et nos arts.
>
> I am much afraid that we shall have very greatly hastened the decline and ruin of this new world by our contagion and *that we will have sold it our opinions and our arts very dear.*[97]
>
> Mais, quant à la devotion, observance des loix, bonté, liberalité, loyauté, franchise, il nous a bien servy de n'en avoir pas tant qu'eux: ils se sont perdus par cet advantage, et vendus, et trahis eux mesme.
>
> But *as for devoutness, observance of the laws, goodness,* liberality, *loyalty,* and *frankness,* it *served us well not to have as much as they: by their advantage in this they lost, sold, and betrayed themselves.*[98]
>
> Combien il eust esté aisé de faire son profit d'ames si neuves, si affamées d'apprentissage, ayant pour la plus part de si beaux commencemens naturels! Au rebours, nous nous sommes servis de leur ignorance et inexperience à les plier plus facilement vers la trahison, luxure, avarice et vers toute sorte d'inhumanité . . . à l'exemple et patron de nos meurs.
>
> How easy it would have been to make good use of souls so fresh . . . having . . . such fine natural beginnings! On the contrary, *we took advantage of their ignorance* and inexperience *to incline them more easily toward treachery* . . . and every sort of inhumanity . . . *after the . . . pattern of our ways.*[99]

Montaigne is clear that "we" triumphed over the new world because "we" were more thoroughly immersed in living outside "ourselves," that is, in employing one another primarily as means instrumental to our purposes and in development of the arts, all of which have their purposes outside themselves : "all art has its end outside itself: *no art is directed to itself.*"[100] This implies that gradually we were conducted out of primitive and childlike wonder at the present moment, into a means-dominated realm of extraneous and future purposes.

Montaigne's observations on the life of kings in the essay "Of the disadvantage of greatness" are very consistent with our characterizations, even largely predictable, but they are worthwhile noting for their explicitness. In brief, Montaigne thinks the life of great kings is a largely unhappy one, with little repose, and one he is happy to avoid, lacking either the taste or capacity for it:

> Le plus aspre et difficile mestier du monde, à mon gré, c'est faire dignement le Roy.... Il est difficile de garder mesure à une puissance si desmesurée.
>
> *The toughest and the most difficult occupation in the world*, in my opinion, *is to play the part of a king worthily.... It is difficult for a power so immoderate to observe moderation.*[101]
>
> ... car, à le prendre exactement, un Roy n'a rien proprement sien; il se doibt soy-mesmes à autruy.
>
> For, to be precise about it, a king has nothing properly his own; *he owes his very self to others.*[102]
>
> ... mais pourtant si ne m'est-il jamais advenu de souhaiter ny empire ny Royauté, ... je m'ayme trop.... Je suis duit à un estage moyen, comme par mon sort, aussi par mon goust.... Je suis degousté de maistrise et active et passive....
>
> ... *it has never occurred to me to wish for empire or royalty ... I love myself too well.... I am trained to a middle station, by my taste as well as by my lot.... I have a dislike for mastery*, both active and passive.[103]

The unhappy aspects of kingly life which Montaigne lists we have seen before: kings constantly wear masks and live outside themselves in the eyes of others; they have no equals whom they can trust for honest and sincere counsel and competition; and they are, by necessity, immersed in the cultivation and manipulation of means and persons for future ends: "Superiority and inferiority of position ... are forced into natural envy and contention; they must pillage one another perpetually."[104] We may note in passing (of which more later) that Jean-Jacques Rousseau subsequently develops these particular Montaignian themes in great detail in his analysis of the alienation of modern, civilized life, brought about in the "slavery" of endless cultivation of means for power over others.

The long essay "Of vanity" provides some refined variation of our central themes. Montaigne sees that it is most appropriate for human beings to turn inward and contemplate themselves, referring to the oracle's counsel at Delphi:

> Sauf toy ô homme, disoit ce Dieu, cháque chose s'estudie la premiere et a, selon son besoin, des limites à ses travaux et desirs. Il n'en est une seule si vuide et necessiteuse que toy, qui embrasses l'univers....
>
> *"Except for you, O man," said the god, "each thing studies itself first, and, according to its needs, has limits to its labors and desires. There is not a single thing as empty and needy as you, who embrace the universe...."*[105]

And he praises (without detectable irony) those few who are truly satisfied with themselves:

> Ceux qui suyvent l'autre extremité, de s'aggreer en eux-mesmes, d'estimer ce qu'ils tiennent au dessus du reste et de ne reconnoistre aucune forme plus belle que celle qu'ils voyent, ... ils sont à la verité plus heureux. Je n'envie poinct leur sagesse, mais ouy leur bonne fortune.
>
> *These who go to the other extreme, of taking delight in themselves, of valuing what they have above other things* and recognizing nothing as more beautiful than what they see ... are in truth happier. I ... envy ... their good fortune.[106]

Yet most human beings are drawn by the vain desire to shine in the eyes of others (another theme subsequently developed by Rousseau):

> Qui que ce soit, ou art ou nature, qui nous imprime cette condition de vivre par la relation à autruy, nous faict beaucoup plus de mal que de bien.... Il ne nous chaut pas tant quel soit nostre estre en nous et en effaict, comme quel il soit en la cognoissance publique.
>
> *Whatever it is, whether art or nature, that imprints in us this disposition to live with reference to others, it does us more harm than good....* We do not care so much what we are in ourselves and in reality as what we are in the public mind. Even the joys of the mind ... appear fruitless to us, if they are enjoyed by ourselves alone, if they do not shine forth to ... the approbation of others.[107]

Montaigne lets us know that he is not immune to the vain and curious temptations to live outside himself—he loves to travel and see new things and peoples; he exaggerates the nobility of his family line; he is proud of the honorary Roman citizenship conferred on him; he has been momentarily tempted by ambition during his private negotiations for kings of France;

and, of course, he publishes his essays—repeatedly. Yet, by and large, Montaigne has been able, both by inclination and lack of innate executive ability, to avoid the slavery of affairs (even those of his own household), the scramble for riches, and ambition for power and reputation, and to live and delight in the present moment:

> Mon dessein est divisible par tout: il n'est pas fondé en grandes esperances; chaque journée en faict le bout. Et le voyage de ma vie se conduict de mesme.
>
> *My plan is everywhere divisible; it is not based on great hopes; each day's journey forms an end.* And the journey of my life is conducted in the same way.[108]

The essay "Of husbanding your will" revisits Montaigne's familiar themes about performing duties to others while being true to oneself and refines it further. Montaigne begins by noting once again the slavery most men are under in devoting their time and attention to others, whether to gain their favor or to maintain their allegiance, or, in rare cases, out of genuine sentiments of self-sacrifice (as in the case of Montaigne's father). Montaigne does not deny that we have obligations to others ("He who lives not at all unto others, hardly lives unto himself"[109]), but thinks it most important for the sake of happiness and tranquillity to meet those obligations moderately, dispassionately, and self-reflectively, reserving the bulk of our energy, time, and attention for that "salutary and well-regulated friendship that each man owes to himself."[110] Here are representative instances of Montaigne's reasoning on what is owed to others and what is owed to oneself.

> La principale charge que nous ayons, c'est à chacun sa conduite; et est ce pourquoy nous sommes icy.
>
> *The main responsibility of each of us is his own conduct;* and that is what we are here for.[111]
>
> La plus part des reigles et preceptes du monde prennent ce train de nous pousser hors de nous et chasser en la place, à l'usage de la societé publique.
>
> *Most of the rules and precepts of the world take this course of pushing us out of ourselves* and . . . *into the market place, for the benefit of society.*[112]
>
> La plus part de nos vacations sont farcesques. . . . Il faut jouer deuement nostre rolle, mais comme rolle d'un personnage emprunté. Du masque et de l'ap-

parence il n'en faut pas faire une essence réelle, ny de l'estranger le propre. . . . Le maire et Montaigne ont tousjour esté deux, d'une separation bien claire.

We must play our part duly, but as the part of a borrowed character. Of the mask and appearance we must not make a real essence, nor of what is foreign what is our very own. . . . *The mayor and Montaigne have always been two, with a very clear separation.*[113]

J'ay peu me mesler des charges publiques sans me despartir de moy. . . . et me donner à autruy sans m'oster à moy.

I have been able to take part in public office without departing . . . from myself, and to give myself to others without taking myself from myself.[114]

To review, Montaigne reasons that tranquillity of soul requires being in control of our conduct as much as possible, and this in turn requires not being possessed or controlled by desires and embroilments which take us outside ourselves and into an instrumental realm most of the time. Montaigne has been able to serve two terms as mayor of Bordeaux and also serve as intermediary for kings and potentates without betraying his own self or "ruling pattern," by being open about his lack of political ambition and executive ability:

A mon arrivée, je me deschiffray fidelement et conscientieusement, tout tel que je me sens estre: sans memoire, sans vigilance, sans experience, et sans vigueur; sans hayne aussi, sans ambition, sans avarice, et sans violence. . . .

On my arrival I deciphered myself to them faithfully . . . such as I feel myself to be: without memory, without vigilance, without experience, and without vigor; also without hate, without ambition, without avarice, and without violence. . . . [115]

In brief, Montaigne performed his public duties as "privately" as possible (something feasible because he had no *very* high or great public responsibilities) in order to remain master of his time and spend it, insofar as possible, in activity for its own sake and in the present moment. And he rejects the supreme sort of self-sacrifice for the public good which ruined his father's health and repose, implying that his father took literally exaggerated precepts of duty which had been crafted by others for public rhetorical purposes:

Il avoit ouy dire qu'il se falloit oublier pour le prochain, que le particulier ne venoit en aucune consideration au pris du general.

> He had heard it said that we must forget ourselves for our neighbor, that the individual was not to be considered at all in comparison with the general.[116]

> Quand ils nous ordonnent d'aymer avant nous . . . cinquante degrez de choses, ils representent l'art des archiers qui, pour arriver au point, vont prenant leur visée grande espace au dessus la bute.

> When they order us to love . . . fifty degrees of things before ourselves, they imitate the techniques of the archers who, to hit the mark, take aim at a great distance above the target.[117]

Montaigne also observes in this connection that to allow oneself to be possessed completely by some public purpose is not as sustainable a way of getting on as detached flexibility:

> Celuy qui n'y employe que son jugement et son adresse, il y procede plus gayement: il feinct, il ploye, il differe tout à son aise, selon le besoing des occasions; . . . prest et entier pour une nouvelle entreprise. . . .

> He who employs in it only his judgment and skill proceeds more gaily. He feints, he bends, he postpones entirely at his ease according to the need of the occasions . . . and remains intact and ready for a new undertaking. . . .[118]

"Of cripples" provides insight into why Montaigne thinks enjoyment of the given, insofar as possible, is the appropriate approach to living. This essay revisits some of the skeptical and Augustinian arguments of "The Apology for Raymond Sebond" about the uncertainty and vagueness of human reason and its inability to unravel the structure of the universe and of human experience:

> La cognoissance des causes appartient seulement à celuy qui a la conduite des choses, non à nous qui n'en avons que la souffrance, et qui en avons l'usage parfaictement plein, selon nostre nature, sans en penetrer l'origine et l'essence.

> The knowledge of causes belongs only to Him who has the guidance of things, not to us who have only the enduring of them, and who have the perfectly full use of them . . . without penetrating to their origin and essence.[119]

Given our limited capacities, Montaigne thinks it appropriate to enjoy and use the things of the world, not attempt to dissect and master them:

> . . . le corps et l'ame interrompent et alterent le droit qu'ils ont de l'usage du monde, y meslant l'opinion de science. Le determiner et le sçavoir, comme le

donner, appartient à la regence et à la maistrise; à l'inferiorite, subjection et apprentissage appartient le jouyr, l'accepter.

... both the body and the soul disturb and alter the right they have to enjoyment of the world by mixing into it the pretension of learning. Determining and knowing, like giving, appertains to rule and mastery; to inferiority ... appertains enjoyment and acceptance.[120]

It is clear from his arguments and examples in this essay and in "Apology for Raymond Sebond" that Montaigne does not foresee as a human possibility the kinds of mastery over physical nature in physics and medicine achieved in the past several centuries by the Cartesian and Baconian project for sure and certain knowledge. Yet Montaigne's arguments about what is appropriate for human beings, given his assessment of human capacities, cannot be dismissed as mistaken until the verdict is in on all the unintended ecological and human consequences of the modern scientific and political project to master nature and human nature through the cumulative fruits of the applied scientific method. Montaigne also uses the skeptical arguments of this essay to encourage greater tolerance and milder punishments for crimes such as witchcraft, about which our knowledge is so vague:

A tuer les gens, il faut une clarté lumineuse et nette; et est nostre vie trop réele et essentielle pour garantir ces accidens supernaturels et fantastiques.

To kill men, we should have sharp and luminous evidence; and our life is too real and essential to vouch for these supernatural and fantastic accidents.[121]

The essay "Of physiognomy" (on the relation of outer form to inner character) gives insight into the reasons for Montaigne's oft-professed candor and openness and his aversion to cultivation and manipulation of complicated instrumental means for his own protection. Montaigne recounts in detail two incidents in his life when men had plans to do him and his estate great harm, and at the last moment relented and gave up these intentions owing, Montaigne believes, in part (the rest is owed to Fortune), to his openness and to his face and demeanor:

Souvant depuis il a dict, ... que mon visage et ma franchise luy avoient arraché la trahison des poincts.

He has often said ... that my face and my frankness had disarmed him of his treachery.[122]

> ... que je devoy cette delivrance à mon visage, liberté et fermeté de mes parolles, qui me rendoyent indigne d'une telle mes-adventure....
>
> ... that I owed my deliverance to my face and the freedom and firmness of my speech, which made me undeserving of such a misadventure...[123]
>
> Si mon visage ne respondoit pour moy, si on ne lisoit en mes yeux et en ma voix la simplicité de mon intention, je n'eusse pas duré sans querelle et sans offence si long temps, avec cette liberté indiscrete de dire à tort et a droict ce qui me vient en fantasie....
>
> ... if people did not read in my eyes and my voice the innocence of my intentions, I would not have lasted so long without quarrel and without harm, considering my indiscreet freedom in saying . . . whatever comes into my head....[124]

In Montaigne's own case, then, the rather direct correspondence between his open inner self and open outer form (in combination with his lack of decisive executive ability) has impelled him to trust Fortune and the good will of others, even those initially bent on doing him harm, rather than attempt to craft competent defenses for himself and his estate. (Unless we follow the unlikely interpretation that Montaigne should not be read at face value, and that, in this case, it was his potential malefactors who were fooled.[125]) Yet Montaigne also observes that such direct correspondence between inner and outer is not always present, citing the inherited accounts of Socrates whose inner beauty was clothed in a face of superficial ugliness. Montaigne confesses that this lack of inner and outer correspondence in the accounts of Socrates "vexes" him, since beauty is such an important quality for him:

> Je ne puis dire assez souvant combien j'estime la beauté, qualité puissante et advantageuse.... Nous n'en avons point qui la surpasse en credit. Elle tient le premier rang au commerce des hommes: elles ... seduict et preoccupe nostre jugement avec grande authorité....
>
> *I cannot say often enough how much I consider beauty a powerful and advantageous quality.* ... *We have no quality that surpasses it in credit. It holds the first place in human relations.* ... *it seduces our judgment with great authority.*...[126]

Yet he consoles himself in the case of Socrates with the observation that although there is some reciprocal connection between the soul and the outer form, superficial ugliness does not influence the spirit in the way actual deformity does. And he goes on in this discussion to suggest that it is ruinous for any society to persuade people that outward religious observance (without morality, without conscience) is enough "to satisfy divine justice."[127] Perhaps, then, judging too much from his own rather unique case (which he elsewhere cautions us not to do[128]), Montaigne counsels general abstention from complicated instrumental plans to secure ourselves against future occurrences:

> Et suis homme en outre qui me commets volontiers à la fortune et me laisse aller à corps perdue enentre ses bras.
>
> I am the sort of man who readily commits himself to Fortune and abandons himself bodily into her arms.[129]
>
> Nous faillons, ce me semble, en ce que nous ne nous fions pas assez au ciel de nous, et pretendons plus de nostre conduite qu'il ne nous appartient. Pourtant fourvoyent si souvent nos desseins. Il est jaloux de l'estenduë que nous attribuons aux droicts de l'humaine prudence . . . et nous les racourcit d'autant que nous les amplifions.
>
> *We err, it seems to me, in that we do not trust ourselves enough to heaven, and we expect more from our own conduct than belongs to us.* That is why our plans so often go astray. *Heaven is jealous* of the extent to which we attribute to the claims of human wisdom . . . and the more we amplify them, the more it cuts them down.[130]

The long (and final) essay of Book III, "Of experience," rehearses a number of themes we have already inspected: the advantages of ordinary life over the life of the great, the wisdom of Socrates, the considered prejudice in favor of existing laws and institutions, the infinite variety of the world, the importance of learning to belong to ourselves well enough to achieve order and tranquillity in our conduct, among others:

> Il n'est rien si beau et legitime que de faire bien l'homme et deuëment, ny science si ardue que de bien et naturellement sçavoir vivre cette vie. . . .
>
> *There is nothing so beautiful and legitimate as to play the man well and properly,* no knowledge as hard to acquire as the knowledge of how to live this life well. . . . [131]

Yet this essay also contains some reflections which explicitly illustrate what I have called Montaigne's "temporal solipsism," or the attempt insofar as possible to delight in the present moment, to the exclusion of future and instrumental considerations. In brief, Montaigne says that we should rush through moments of intense pain (mild pain can actually be a stimulus for self-inspection) and savor pleasurable moments, but never simply "pass the time":

> Il faut courir le mauvais et se rassoir au bon. Cette fraze ordinaire de passetemps et de passer le temps represente l'usage de ces prudentes gens, qui ne pensent point avoir meilleur compte de leur vie que de la couler et eschapper, de la passer, ... Mais je la cognois autre.... «*Stulti vita ingrata est, trepida est, tota in futurum fertur.*»

> *We must run through the bad and settle on the good. This ... expression "pastime" ... represents the habit of those ... folk who think they can make no better use of their life than to let it slip by.... But I know it to be otherwise.... We have only ourselves to blame if it weighs on us and escapes us unprofitably. The life of the fool is joyless, full of trepidation, given over wholly to the future.* [Seneca]¹³²

> Je consulte d'un contentement avec moy, je ne l'escume pas; ... Me trouve-je en quelque assiete tranquille? y a il quelque volupté qui me chatouille? je ne la laisse pas friponer aux sens, j'y associe mon ame, non pas pour s'y engager, mais pour s'y agreer, non pas pour s'y perdre, mais pour s'y trouver; ... combien luy vaut d'estre logèe en tel point que, où qu'elle jette sa veuë, le ciel est calme autour d'elle: nul desir, nulle crainte ou doubte qui luy trouble l'air, aucune difficulté passée, presente, future....

> *I meditate over any satisfaction; I do not skim over it ... Is there some ... pleasure that tickles me? I do not let my senses pilfer it, I bring my soul into it ... to enjoy herself, not to lose herself but to find herself ... how much it is worth to her to be lodged at such a point that wherever she casts her eyes ... no difficulty, past, present or future....* ¹³³

This essay also contains the single thought which might be called the key to Montaigne's art of living:

> Nostre grand et glorieux chef-d'œuvre c'est vivre à propos. Toutes autres choses, regner, thesauriser, bastir, n'en sont qu'appendicules et adminicules pour le plus.

> *Our great and glorious masterpiece is to live appropriately. All other things, ruling, hoarding, building, are only little appendages and props at most.*¹³⁴

We have seen that for Montaigne "living appropriately" (after much self-exploration) means living as private a life as possible (even in his public duties), for this choice affords him the greatest latitude to do things for their own sake, treat other human beings as ends and not mere means, and delight in the present moment as much as possible. It is only for a few truly great souls such as Alexander or Caesar to "live appropriately" by taking on great projects in the world, for only the great can rise above the tyranny of instrumentality in huge enterprises, and continue to do them (and other things) for their own sake:

> C'est aux petites ames, ensepvelies du pois des affaires, de ne s'en sçavoir purement desmesler, de ne les sçavoir et laisser et reprendre. . . .
>
> It is for little souls, buried under the weight of business, to be unable to detach themselves clearly from it or to leave it and pick it up again. . . . [135]

And Montaigne permits himself the thought here at the end of his book that there is a kind of greatness of soul in any mixture of body and soul coming to understand itself, to know its limits, and to "live appropriately," given the difficulty of this undertaking.

Before attempting a measured appraisal of Montaigne's "art of living" in the *Essais*, it is enlightening to inspect two of his central ideas as developed by two subsequent thinkers, Jean-Jacques Rousseau and Michael Oakeshott. The point in these excursions is not to show intellectual influence but to gain appreciation of the importance of themes which Montaigne does not analyze in detail, given the style of his expression, and the fact that he is not writing treatises. Let us look first at Rousseau's development of the Montaignian theme that much of our activity and energy is a form of slavery to others.

Although this theme is stated in the famous second sentence of the first chapter of *The Social Contract* ("one thinks himself the master of others, and still remains a greater slave than they"[136]), it is developed in two earlier works, "A Discourse on the Origins of Inequality" and "A Discourse on the Moral Effects of the Arts and Sciences." These essays attempt to show that the "fall of man" into the main realm of accumulating means to increase power and status has led not to aggregate increased happiness but to discontent and moral corruption, based on extreme dependency on the opinions of others. (The theme that human beings be viewed first and foremost as creators of means for future purposes and power is, of course, already in the social philosophy of Thomas Hobbes, but Hobbes simply views this as the inescapable human condition.)

These Rousseauan themes have been aptly summarized and drawn out by Arthur Melzer in his book *The Natural Goodness of Man: On the System of Rousseau's Thought*. Since we are looking for an encapsulated account of Rousseau's teaching on this score for purposes of drawing out the importance of Montaigne's views, let us go directly to Melzer's summary formulation of Rousseau on the tyranny of the world of instrumental means:

> But men, as soon as their minds develop, begin to turn their attention to the pursuit of "means," of things not good in themselves, but useful for the acquisition of future goods. This indirect approach to the satisfaction of our desires is capable of taking on a life of its own, alienating us from our true needs and from ourselves.[137]

> The problem with external means is . . . that . . . using them involves at least a momentary abandonment of our natural inclination . . . while we obey the laws that govern the functioning of the means. To control, we must obey. As technology becomes more complex . . . this "obedience to means" begins seriously to compromise our freedom and unity. . . . The power needed to acquire, protect, and use a means is often greater than . . . the power one acquires from the means . . . so that the acquisition of means . . . actually increase one's need for power.[138]

> The contradiction of power does not fully come into play . . . unless the means we seek to use are human beings, the most uncontrollable of all objects. "Nothing is less stable among men," Rousseau insists, "than those external relationships which are called weakness or power, wealth or poverty."[139]

> Only by an all-consuming and endless attention to others can one succeed in getting them to serve oneself.[140]

This insightful analysis of the implications of Rousseau's teaching on the human alienation involved in the cultivation of both technological and human means for the accumulation of power and status (owing to the continual and time-consuming need for more power) is also useful in showing the continued importance and relevance of both Montaigne's and Rousseau's views on their subjects. For as generally formulated by Melzer—the idea that cultivation of external means for power and status takes on an all-consuming life of its own—this analysis is as easily recognizable as apt for our own time, if not more so,[141] than for that of Montaigne and Rousseau.

Another subsequent thinker whose development and amplification of a Montaignian theme highlights its importance and relevance is the twentieth-century English philosopher Michael Oakeshott. The theme in question is the orientation to live and delight as much in the present moment as is possible and appropriate, given the dissatisfaction inherent in performing actions for future purposes.

Oakeshott's description of the "conversative disposition" in the well-known essay "On being conversative" is reminiscent of Montaigne (whom Oakeshott thought a remarkable individual):

> The general characteristics of this disposition . . . centre upon a prosperity to use and enjoy what is available . . . to delight in what is present rather than what was or what may be . . .[142]

> *To be conservative, then, is . . . to prefer the* tried to the untried, fact to mystery, the actual to the possible, the limited to the unbounded, the near to the distant . . . *the convenient to the perfect, present laughter to utopian bliss.* Familiar relationships and loyalties will be preferred . . . *to acquire and to enlarge will be less important than to . . . cultivate and enjoy . . . It is to be equal to one's own fortune . . .* to be content with the want of greater perfection which belongs alike to oneself and one's circumstances.[143]

And here is Oakeshott from a different essay on the emptiness and futility of cultivation of instrumental means for future purposes, such as a "career":

> *Ambition and the world's greed for results would be superseded by a life which carried in each of its moments its whole meaning and value. For, after all, could any notion of life be more empty and futile than this idea that its value is measured by its contribution to something more permanent than itself*—a race, a people, an art, a science, or a profession, *this is surely to preach an illusive immortality.*[144]

Although Oakeshott always pursues the logical implications of his views further and more purely than Montaigne, that is precisely their usefulness for our purposes in focusing on the importance of Montaigne's themes. The similarities to Montaigne's in these Oakeshottian views are strong and apparent, as is Oakeshott's approach to taking delight in the present, that is, doing activities for their own sake where appropriate. Oakeshott distinguishes between activities and relationships in which it is appropriate "merely to enjoy what they offer for its own sake,"[145] and those where it is more appropriate to seek some substantive result or service, as in relationships between buyers and sellers or clients and lawyers. He suggests that in these latter kinds of relationships the disposition merely to enjoy what is present to the exclusion of satisfying some want is an irrational inclination, though he does observe (calling to mind Montaigne's attempt to perform public duties in as "private" a manner possible) that reducing such relationships to mere mechanical functions seems inappropriate as well:

> *Though even these relationships seem to lack something appropriate* to them *when* they are confined to a nexus of supply and demand and *allow no room for the intrusion of the loyalties and attachments which spring from familiarity.*[146]

As instances of the other kind of relationship—"in which no result is sought and which are engaged in for their own sake and enjoyed for what they are and not what they provide"—Oakeshott suggests friendship, conversation, patriotism (distinguished from utilitarian calculations of private benefit for public service), and fishing (where it is not one's livelihood). Oakeshott's account of these activities is logically "purer" than Montaigne's, systematically excluding any substantive consideration from them (such as pursuit of truth in conversation or mutual improvement in friendship), but there is a similarity in their approaches which Oakeshott characteristically makes more explicit than does Montaigne, yet which I believe is present in Montaigne's sensibilities as well and which becomes more apparent after reading Oakeshott. This similarity is the appreciation of the importance of ritual and ritualistic practices in the daily achievement of human repose because of the familiarity which they provide (Montaigne says that he would rather say the Lord's Prayer a hundred times than a new prayer), and for the release they provide from concern about achievement and success in the external world. Oakeshott makes explicit the point about ritual in a brief discussion of fishing:

> *But fishing is an activity that may be engaged in,* not for the profit of a catch, but *for its own sake; and the fisherman may return home in the evening not less content for being empty-handed. Where this is so, the activity has become a ritual.* . . . What matters is the enjoyment of exercising skill (or, perhaps, merely passing the time). . . . [147]

Oakeshott makes other connections in the essay "On being conservative" which Montaigne does not make explicit, but which buttress and amplify

Montaigne's views on the importance of custom, tradition, and the dangers of innovation in government. In brief, Oakeshott observes that it is supremely appropriate and even efficient to be "conservative or familiar with the tools we use, and the rules of conduct and routines we follow, because their familiarity and predictability is exactly what we value in them, and the burden of proof should be on proposed innovation for improvement to show conclusively that it can live up to its promise before it be adopted."[148]

Let us conclude this excursion into Oakeshott's thought by putting in perspective themes I have developed at length elsewhere.[149] In my view Oakeshott and Montaigne have both drawn on the Augustinian-Trinitarian criticism of the classical dualism of Plato and Aristotle for its failure to see that there is nothing inherently corrupting or fatal in matter[150] and that there is no hiatus in the human being between body and soul, between sense impression and thought. For this reason, in the views of Montaigne and Oakeshott there are activities which can be done for their own sake, and enjoyed for their own sake in the present moment, other than *Theoria*, or thought thinking thought. In Augustine's view, time, space, matter, and form are not merely hindrances and "causes," but gifts or opportunities for individual self-enactment and disclosure in the secular realm, and it is toward the meaning of human conduct that the limited reasoning power of a creature of body and soul immersed in time should properly be directed, not toward questions of scientific causality. Here is Oakeshott putting this viewpoint in secular terms, a viewpoint dramatically implied in Montaigne's cultivation of himself in the *Essais*:

> *What has to be reckoned with is an historic disposition* to transform this unsought freedom of conduct from a postulate into an experience and to make it yield a satisfaction of its own . . . *the disposition to recognize imagining, deliberating, wanting, choosing and acting not as costs incurred in seeking enjoyments, but as themselves enjoyments, the exercise of a gratifying self-determination or personal antonomy.*[151]

Before finally coming to a recapitulation and assessment of Montaigne's "art of living," it is also useful for further perspective to contrast his views with two subsequent, avowed foes of individuality and the "inner Augustinian personality," Karl Marx and John Dewey. We have seen throughout the *Essais* Montaigne's preference for viewing individuals in terms of their uniqueness and by the standards of each's own interior governing pattern or form *(forme maistresse)*. Here is one of the more explicit instances from the essay "Of Cato the younger":

> Je n'ay point cette erreur commune de juger d'un autre selon que je suis. . . . Je . . . le considere simplement en luy-mesme, sans relation, l'estoffant sur son propre modelle. . . . Je desire singulierement qu'on nous juge chascun à part soy, et qu'on ne me tire en consequence des communs exemples.
>
> I do not share that common error of judging another by myself. . . . *I consider him simply in himself, without relation to others; I mold him to his own model.* . . . I have the singular desire that we should each be judged in ourselves apart, and that I may not be measured in conformity with the common patterns.[152]

Montaigne's view of the importance of unique, interior individual standards is in stark contrast to the subsequent view of Marx and Dewey that society does not consist of individuals but of their interrelations and that what is important about a person and defines the person are the relations with other persons. Here is John Dewey on this point in his influential 1916 work, *Democracy and Education:*

> What is called inner is simply that which does not connect with others—what is not capable of free and full communication. *What is termed spiritual culture has usually been futile with something rotten about it, just because it has been conceived as a thing which a man might have internally—and therefore exclusively. What one is as a person is what one is associated with others.*[153]

One cannot imagine a view more antithetical to Montaigne's than this statement of Dewey, but it is useful by contrast in indicating the importance of Montaigne's largely implicit defense of individuality. For Montaigne is not praising individuality in the manner of the Protestant divines (whom he opposes) who argued that the individual was superior to the community in one important respect—the ability to know God (as in the counsel, "be still and hear the voice of God"). We have seen that for Montaigne religion was largely a matter of public ritual, not interior conscience. Nor does the skeptical Montaigne articulate a conception of natural rights of personality as the subsequent fathers of classical liberalism did. Rather, Montaigne implicitly defends the importance and uniqueness of his own individual self simply because it is his. In terms of scholastic philosophy, Montaigne implies that the accidents of his particular existence are a constitutive part of his essence, not deviations from a putative, perfect personality, and they are also more important in defining him than abstract relations with other selves in a largely externalized and transparent set of social relations (as in Marx's and Dewey's view).

Let us try now for a recapitulation and assessment of Montaigne's "art of living." The first or grounding feature of Montaigne's orientation to be observed is that its overriding consideration is the repose, tranquillity, and balance or harmony of the mixture of body and soul (and its various and conflicting impulses, desires, and aspirations) which make up Montaigne. There are other possible orientations which come to mind by contrast—for instance, the intent to follow precepts of duty for their own sake, or to follow a divine or secular law or code to the letter for its own sake, or to follow the pursuit of scientific causality with all one's time and energy, or the pursuit of some sensual pleasure or appetite to the exclusion of all else, and so on.

The goal of repose, in turn, requires, in Montaigne's view, mastery of the fear of death and avoidance of severe pain where possible for most people, including Montaigne. It also requires as accurate an appraisal as possible of one's strengths and limits and a discernment of one's interior ruling form (*une forme maistresse*), as a step in "appropriate living." Appropriate living, in turn, requires doing things insofar as possible for their own sake and in the present moment rather than as instrumental means for future purposes. For Montaigne, and all but a few truly great souls, doing things for their own sake requires living a largely private life, filled with private rituals and activities such as conversation and friendship. (Public duties are performed, in turn, in as "private a manner" as possible.) The limits of human reason and the tyranny of a life of instrumental means (as, for instance, in a high political career) also suggest the prudence in following whenever possible inherited political and religious rituals and customs in lieu of pursuing innovation.

It would appear that Montaigne's "art of living" was certainly suitable for himself, given his own proclivities and limits. An orientation to delight in the present moment whenever possible makes good sense in the case of a personality made up of a surprising number of contrarieties, living in a time of vast civil upheaval, possessed of a poor memory, lacking decisive executive capacities, and with the inherited financial resources to sustain and make viable a largely private life (even while performing unavoidable political obligations). The interesting question is whether this approach to living makes sense for others as well. This question can be taken on *both* a personal *and* a broad political and cultural level.

Although Montaigne often cautions us not to judge what is possible by our own capacities, in one important respect it would seem that he does just this. Montaigne's own personality would appear to have been so highly variable (recall he does not portray himself, only his "passage" from moment to moment), that except for very rare individuals, such as Alexander and Cato, he does not see enough constancy in the human character for it to achieve satisfaction in a life of practical purposes. Nor does he appear to have envisioned as a distinct human possibility the kind of constancy in accumulation of data and control over physical nature which the Cartesian and Baconian scientific project has been able to achieve thus far. (As we've already noted, however, Montaigne's assessment of the ultimate futility of this kind of project cannot be dismissed.) We can observe, though, that it may have been a blindness on Montaigne's part concerning the degree of satisfaction (if not repose) which large numbers of ordinary individuals might find in pursuit of public and practical purposes, even ones immersed in the realm of instrumentality. Moreover, as a strategy for escaping the "deadliness of doing," that is, the alienation of a life devoted to cultivation of instrumental means, delight in the present moment has long been a human insight and is evident especially in the reflections of Horace and Seneca. And the view that the limits of time-bound human reason make it more suitable for inspection of human meaning than for investigation of ultimate causes is clearly present in the thought of Augustine. And Aristotle and other ancient philosophers speak of activities done for their own sake. What is new and also still relevant in Montaigne's reflections?

In my view, Montaigne's orientation toward living "appropriately" may be seen most coherently as employing various insights (when appropriate) of ancient thinkers—the Skeptics, the Stoics, Plato and Xenophon on Socrates, the Roman pastoral poets, St. Augustine—to suit his own purposes, to accommodate his own strengths and weaknesses, his own *"master form."* In so doing, Montaigne implicitly gives us in the *Essais* a new and unique (for the sixteenth century) synthesis of ancient Greco-Roman, Christian, and Renaissance-humanist ideas about appropriate living. From ancient Greek philosophers, he takes the importance in human fulfillment of doing things for their own sake where intelligently possible; from Christianity and Stoicism, the insight to look at the world differently or in a different light through an act of will; from himself, an instinctive appreciation of the sheer diversity and uniqueness in the world; and he puts it all together in a point of view which sees that it is possible to do many things for their own sake (besides simply *Theoria*), simply by looking at them uninstrumentally and in a new light.

We have seen that there are limits in public and practical life to acting uninstrumentally toward things and other people, but that Montaigne resolved to perform public duties in as "private" a manner as possible and was generally successful at it by being open about his lack of political ambition and by occupying and performing only intermediate positions and tasks. By living a largely private life, Montaigne was able to devote himself to cultivating activities such as self-exploration, conversation, and friendship, which could be done for their own sake and in the present moment. The self-exploration also led Montaigne to a defense of his own individuality (which was new and has been influential) simply on the grounds it was uniquely his, and that was its importance. Yet in qualifying this uniqueness by putting it in the context of an appreciation of limited human powers and hence of the importance of established customs and practices, he avoided the kind of anarchically willful individualism characteristic of later Romantics and of the nineteenth-century thinker Friedrich Nietzsche, and achieved "an aristocratic sense of his own unimportance,"[154] an insight arguably as relevant for other times and persons as for Montaigne himself.

CHAPTER III

Montaigne's Religious Views

Montaigne's religious views, especially as laid out in the very long essay "Apology for Raymond Sebond," have been a source of controversy from the sixteenth century to the present. The spectrum of opinion ranges from the view that Montaigne is an atheist maliciously undermining the very religion he purports to defend to the view that he is a devout, practicing Catholic providing a serious defense against Protestant doctrines about the importance of each believer reading and judging Holy Scripture according to his or her own lights. Certainly, part of the adventure of reading the "Apology" (and the other essays) is to decide for oneself where Montaigne stood on the religious questions of God's nature and existence and of the soundness of Roman Catholic dogma. My own view is that an exploration of Montaigne's conception of a distant, unchanging God, and its logical implication for human believers, can go some way in explaining the more "hedonistic" aspects of Montaigne's outlook, without predominant recourse to claims of authorial deception and irony.

By way of exploring those issues, let us look in detail at the structure and arguments of the "Apology for Raymond Sebond," an essay of some 150 pages in the Frame translation, written between 1575 and 1580, ostensibly defending the views of a book on natural theology by a Spanish writer who attempted to show that natural reason and observation of the world supported the Christian revelation. (Montaigne had earlier translated the book from Latin at the request of his father and apparently wrote this essay at the request of a lady, probably Margaret of Valois, later queen to Henry IV.) The essay doesn't spend much time on Sebond and at one level actually undermines Sebond's thesis by undermining the capacities of human knowledge, but it is useful for our purpose in coming to some provisional judgments on Montaigne's religious beliefs. I believe a systematic exploration of the essay gives a better picture of Montaigne's religious beliefs than would selective quotation drawn from throughout the *Essais*. In brief, this essay tries to establish the necessity for human reliance on faith and on God's grace by recalling human beings to their "littleness"—by reminding them of the modesty of their natural talents, especially intellectual ones. It also provides a classical, Plutarchian conception of God as a distant, unchanging, and timeless being, a rather impersonal conception, as we shall see, which by implication leaves human beings considerable latitude and discretion in the conduct of their daily lives.

Montaigne begins fairly early on by abandoning the defense of Sebond's explicit project and embarking on his own, the strategy for which he lays out explicitly:

> Le moyen que je prens . . . c'est de froisser et fouler aux pieds l'orgueil et humaine fierté; leur faire sentir . . . la vanité et deneantise de l'homme; leur arracher des points les chetives armes de leur raison; leur faire baisser la teste et mordre la terre soubs l'authorité et reverance de la majesté divine.
>
> The means I take . . . is to crush and trample underfoot human arrogance and pride; to make them feel the . . . vanity and nothingness of man; *to wrest from their hands the puny weapons of their reason*; to make them bow their heads . . . beneath the authority and reverence of divine majesty.[1]

Because our reason is so weak and incapable of investigating its own origins and those of our religion, we are thrown back on faith and grace:

> C'est la foy seule qui embrasse vivement et certainement les hauts mysteres de nostre Religion.
>
> It is faith alone that embraces *vividly* and surely the high mysteries of our religion.[2]
>
> Le neud qui devroit attacher nostre jugement et nostre volonté, qui devroit . . . joindre à nostre createur, ce devroit estre un neud prenant ses repliz et ses forces, non pas de nos considerations, de noz raisons et passions, mais d'une estreinte divine et supernaturelle, n'ayant qu'une forme . . . qui est l'authorité de Dieu et sa grace. Or, nostre coeur et nostre ame estant regie et commandée par la foy. . . .

> The knot that should bind our judgment and our will, that should . . . join our soul to our creator, should be a knot taking its . . . strength not from our considerations, our reasons . . . but from a divine and supernatural clasp, . . . which is the authority of God and his grace. *Now, our heart and soul being ruled and commanded by faith.* . . .[3]

Montaigne next proceeds to create the impression of the vanity of human knowledge without God through the use of tropes or techniques for "suspending judgment," which he has borrowed from the ancient Greek Skeptics, in particular Book I, chapters 13 and 14, of Sextus Empiricus's *Outlines of Pyrrhonism*.[4] The first of these tropes is used to puncture human arrogance and vanity for separating itself as superior to other creatures and daring to think itself on occasion as equal to God. Montaigne takes the reader through a tour (over some thirty pages in the Frame edition) of stories and comparisons designed to induce doubt about the superiority of humans to the beasts by indicating their similarities. The reasoning in these is often either weak or fantastic; whatever effect they have comes from the sheer number of them. Here are some representative ones, which attempt to create doubt about the perceived inability of the beasts to reason and speak.

> Ce defaut qui empesche la communication d'entre elles et nous, pourquoy n'est il aussi bien à nous qu'a elles? C'est à deviner, à qui est la faute de ne nous entendre point: car nous ne les entendons non plus qu'elles nous. Par cette mesme raison, elles nous peuvent estimer bestes, comme nous les en estimons.

> This defect that hinders communication between them and us, why is it not just as much ours as theirs? It is a matter of guesswork whose fault it is that we do not understand one another. . . . By the same reasoning, they may consider us beasts, as we consider them.[5]

> Quant au parler, . . . nature . . . a donné à plusieurs autres animaux: car qu'est-ce autre chose que parler, cette faculté que nous leur voyons de se plaindre, de se resjouyr, de s'entr'appeller au secours, se convier à l'amour, comme ils font par l'usage de leur voix? . . . Lactance attribuë aux bestes, non le parler seulement, mais le rire encore.

> As for speech. . . . Nature has given to many animals: for what is it but speech, this faculty we see in them of complaining, rejoicing, calling to each other for help, inviting each other to love, as they do by the use of their voice? . . . Lanctantus attributes to beasts not only speech but also laughter.[6]

Je dy donc ... qu'il n'y a point d'apparence d'estimer que les bestes facent par inclination naturelle. ... les mesmes choses que nous faisons par nostre choix. ... Nous devons conclurre de pareils effects pareilles facultez. ... Par ainsi, le renard ... de passer par dessus la glace quelque riviere gelée ... quand nous le verrions au bord de l'eau approcher son oreille bien pres de la glace, pour sentir s'il orra d'une longue ou d'une voisine distance bruyre l'eau courant au dessoubs, et selon qu'il trouve par là qu'il y a plus ou moins d'espesseur en la glace, se reculer ou s'avancer, n'aurions nous pas raison de juger qu'il luy passe par la teste ce mesme discours qu'il feroit en la nostre, et que c'est une ratiocination. ...

So I say ... *that there is no apparent reason to judge that the beasts do by ... obligatory instinct the same thing we do by choice. ... We must infer from like results like faculties. ... Take the example of the fox ... to cross some frozen stream over the ice. ... If we saw him at the edge of the water bring his ear very near to the ice, to hear whether the water running beneath sounds near or far away, and draw back or advance according as he finds the ice too thin or thick enough, would we not have reason to suppose that there passes through his head the same reasoning that would pass through ours, and that this is ratiocination. ...*[7]

Chrysippus ... considerant les mouvements du chien qui, se recontrant en un carrefour à trois chemins ... il est contraint de confesser qu'en ce chien là un tel discours se passe: J'ay suivy jusques à ce carre-four mon maistre à la trace; il faut necessairement qu'il passe par l'un de ces trois chemins; ce n'est ny par cettuy-cy, ny par celuy-là; il faut donc infailliblement qu'il passe par cet autre; et que, s'asseurant par cette conclusion et discours, il ne se sert plus de son sentiment au troisiesme chemin, ny ne le sonde plus, ains s'y laisse emporter par la force de la raison.

Chrysippus ... considering the movements of *a dog, who, coming upon a crossroads with three roads* ... is forced to confess that in the dog some such reasoning takes place: "... my master ... must necessarily be going by one of these three roads; it is not by this one or that one, so he must ... be going by this other"; and that *assured by this inference and reasoning, he no longer uses this sense of smell on the third road, but lets himself be swept on by the force of his reason. ...*[8]

Montaigne also observes that animals appear to be capable of religion and divination:

Nous pouvons aussi dire que les elephans ont quelque participation de religion, d'autant qu'apres plusieurs ablutions et purifications on les void, haussant leur trompe comme des bras et tenant les yeux fichez vers le Soleil

> levant, se planter long temps en meditation et contemplation a certaines heures du jour, de leur propre inclination, sans instruction. . . .
>
> *We can also say that elephants have some participation in religion,* since after many ablutions and purifications we see them raising their trunks like arms and keeping their eyes fixed toward the rising sun, stand still a long time in meditation and contemplation . . . by their own inclination, without instruction. . . .[9]

He goes on with many other illustrations to suggest that animals are more self-controlled; surpass us in domestic management; are more faithful and less treacherous by far; are capable of mutual assistance societies; and are capable of magnanimity, repentance, clemency, nobility, science, and wisdom. He concludes that

> La maniere de naistre, d'engendrer, nourrir, agir, mouvoir, vivre et mourir des bestes estant si voisine de la nostre, tout ce que nous retranchons de leurs causes motrices et que nous adjoustons à nostre condition au dessus de la leur, cela ne peut aucunement partir du discours de nostre raison.
>
> *Since animals are born, beget, feed, act, move, live and die in a manner so close to our own,* all that we detract from their motive powers, and all that we add to ours to raise our state above theirs, can in no way proceed from the judgment of our reason.[10]

And he suggests that human vanity and arrogance will presently declare that "God himself to make himself appreciated, must resemble us. . . ."[11] We may also note here that throughout this discussion, Montaigne is silent on the biblical account that human beings were made in the image of God (by virtue of their ability to reason about his commandments) and were given dominion over the beasts and fish and fowl of the earth.

Montaigne's next move in the essay is to imply that human knowledge can by itself make us neither content nor good. His arguments vary from among the claims that philosophic knowledge does not exempt one from life's discomforts, nor make sensual pleasure and health more "savory"; that there are more good men among the ignorant than among the learned; and that this truth is borne out in the superiority of old Rome to learned Rome.

> J'en diray seulement encore cela, que c'est la seule humilité et submission qu peut effectuer un homme de bien. Il ne faut pas laisser au jugement de chaucun la cognoissance de son devoir; il le luy faut prescrire, non pas le laisser

choisir à son discours ... d'autant que l'obeyr est le principal office d'une ame raisonnable, recognoissant un celeste superieur. ...

I will add only this, that humility and submissiveness alone can make a good man. The knowledge of his duty should not be left to each man's judgment; it should be prescribed to him, not left to the choice of his reason ... since to obey is the principal function of a reasonable soul, recognizing a heavenly superior. ...[12]

Montaigne continues in this vein by suggesting that philosophic knowledge may actually contribute to our torments, by exciting the imagination and adding to our pain in anticipation of it and by supporting the proximity of the "lusty flights" of the philosophic mind to a subtle madness: "Countless minds have been ruined by their very power and suppleness."[13]

On the point that knowledge cannot make us good, Montaigne's arguments are largely Christian, with the exception of the case of Socrates, whose wisdom was the knowledge of his ignorance. Montaigne cites the biblical account of the fall of man through curiosity and desire for knowledge and says that the participation we have in the knowledge of truth is a gift of faith, which is not of our own acquiring and which is aided more by our blindness than our clear-sightedness:

Ce n'est pas par discours ou par nostre entendement que nous avons receu nostre religion. ... C'est par l'entremise de nostre ignorance plus que de nostre science que nous sommes sçavan de ce divin sçavoir.

It is not by reasoning or by our understanding that we have received our religion. ... It is by the mediation of our ignorance more than our knowledge that we are learned with that divine learning.[14]

He concludes this very Pauline and Augustinian argument with a quote from Corinthians I: "For after the world by wisdom knew not God, it pleased God by the foolishness of preaching to save them that believe."[15]

Montaigne next embarks on a long series of arguments questioning the adequacy of all human knowledge: "Yet I must see at least whether it is in the power of man to find what he seeks, and whether that quest ... has enriched him with ... any solid truth." And he gives us his conclusion before the demonstration: "I think he will confess to me, if he speaks in all conscience, *that all the profit he has gained for so long a pursuit is to have learned to acknowledge his weakness.*"[16]

Montaigne proposes to investigate the accounts of the most "excellent and select" men, a small number of philosophers, whom he divides into three types—those who say they have found what they were searching for (the Peripatetics, Epicureans, Stoics); those who say they have not (the Academics); and those who say they are still searching for the truth (Pyrrho and other Skeptics). Montaigne is clearly most sympathetic to the Skeptic school, and it is instructive to look at his characterization of their viewpoints and rhetorical techniques for suspending judgment, since we must consider the possibility that Montaigne himself throughout the *Essais* is employing these techniques at least some of the time. Montaigne says that the Skeptics or Pyrrhonians mildly search out contradiction and "advance their propositions only to combat those they think we believe in":

> Si vous prenez la leur, ils prendront aussi volontiers la contraire à soustenir: tout leur est un. . . . Oui, et si, par un axiome affirmatif, vous asseurez que vous en doutez, ils vous iront debattant que vous nien doutez pas. . . . Et, par cette extremité de doute qui se secoue soy-mesme, ils se separent et se divisent de plusieurs opinions. . . .
>
> *If you accept their proposition, they will just as gladly take the opposite one to maintain; it is all one to them. . . . Yes, and if by an affirmative action you assure them that you are in doubt about it, they will go and argue that you are not. . . . And by the extremity of doubt that shakes its own foundations, they separate and divide themselves from many opinions. . . .* [17]

Concerning the disputes of the "dogmatists" (such as Aristotle), Montaigne characterizes the Skeptic view thus:

> Vaut il pas mieux demeurer en suspens que de s'infrasquer en tant d'erreurs que l'humaine fantaisie a produictes? Vaut-il pas mieux suspendre sa persuasion que de se mesler à ces divisions seditieuses et quereleuses?
>
> Is it not better to remain in suspense than to entangle yourself in the many errors that human fancy has produced? *Is it not better to suspend your conviction than to get mixed up in these seditious and quarrelsome divisions?* [18]

After characterizing the Skeptic attempt as a perpetual suspension of belief ("they use their reason to inquire and debate, but not to conclude or choose") through the perpetual juxtaposition of contraries, Montaigne takes up their approach to the actions of life, which comes down to being guided by custom and moderate indulgence of appetite without taking sides or making judgments:

> Quant aux actions de la vie. . . . Ils se prestent et accommodent aux inclinations naturelles, a l'impulsion et contrainte des passions, aux constitutions des loix et des coustumes et à la tradition des arts.
>
> As for the actions of life . . . [t]hey . . . accommodate themselves to the natural inclinations, to the impulsion and constraint of the appetites, to the constitutions of laws and customs, and to the tradition of the arts.[19]

Montaigne then defends the Pyrrhonian attitude for its versimilitude and usefulness to a life based on faith:

> Cette-cy presente l'homme nud et vuide . . . propre à recevoir d'en haut quelque force estrangere . . . aneantissant son jugement pour faire plus de place à la foy; ny mescreant, ny establissant aucun dogme contre les observances communes; humble, obeïssant . . . ennemi juré d'haeresie. . . . C'est une carte blance preparée à prendre du doigt de Dieu telles formes qu'il luy plaira y graver.
>
> *It presents man naked and empty* . . . fit to receive from above some outside power . . . *annihilating his judgment to make room for faith;* neither disbelieving nor setting up any doctrine against the common observances; humble, obedient . . . a sworn enemy of heresy. . . . *He is a blank tablet prepared to take from the finger of God such forms as he shall be pleased to engrave on it.*[20]

At this point, we can observe that Montaigne does appear to imply that "the common observances" of Catholic France reflect the forms of God's "engraving," and not some other religious observances. Or, alternatively, Montaigne himself could be following the Skeptic technique of juxtaposing contrary arguments to engender a state of suspended judgment in the reader. Or, alternatively, Montaigne could be engaging in a self-experiment (in the interest of discovery) to let his mind go indifferently wherever impulse and habit take it. We shall try to sort out these possibilities later on.

To return to the argument of "the Apology," we next see Montaigne critique the views of those philosophers he calls the "dogmatists." There are many varied critiques over many pages, but here are some representatives ones. Montaigne calls Aristotle the "prince of the dogmatists" and criticizes him for piling up in his discussions great numbers of opinions and beliefs of others "to compare with his own and show us how much further he has gone," but says that what we actually learn from him is "that knowing much gives occasion for doubting more."[21] In fact, Montaigne says that

Aristotle often hides his own opinions in a "thick and inextricable obscurity," and that his form of argument is "in fact a Pyrrhonism in an affirmative form." Montaigne also suggests more than once (echoing Plato of the "Seventh Letter") that these actual doctrines of Aristotle and Plato and others were for public consumption or were more games for intellectual exercise than anything serious:

> Je ne me persuade pas aysement qu'Epicurus, Platon et Pythagoras nous ayent donné pour argent contant leurs Atoms, leurs Idées et leurs Nombres. Ils estoient trop sages pour establir leurs articles de foy de chose si incertaine et si debatable. . . . et ont promené leur ame à des inventions qui eussent au moins une plaisante et subtile apparence. . . . Aucunes choses, ils les ont escrites pour le besoin de la société publique, comme leurs religions; et a esté raisonnable, pour cette consideration, que les communes opinions ils n'ayent voulu les espelucher au vif aux fins. . . .
>
> *I cannot easily persuade myself that Epicurus, Plato, and Pythagoras gave us their Atoms, their Ideas, and their Numbers as good coin of the realm. They were too wise to establish these articles of faith on anything so uncertain and so debatable. . . . they exercised their minds on such conceptions as had a pleasant . . . appearance. . . . Some things they wrote for the needs of society, like their religions, and on this account it was reasonable that they did not want to bare popular opinions to the bone. . . .* [22]

Montaigne moves on to critique the futility of ancient attempts to know the divinity, citing as the most probable and excusable that "which recognized God as an incomprehensible power, origin and preserver of all things, all goodness, and all perfection," suggesting that God in his mercy, perhaps decided "to foster by these temporal beliefs the tender beginnings of a rough knowledge of him, however feeble":

> . . . celle là me semble avoir eu plus de vray-semblance et plus d'excuse, qui reconnoissoit Dieu comme une puissance incomprehensible, origine et conservatrice de toutes choses, toute bonté, toute perfection. . . . Dieu, par sa misericorde, daignant a l'avanture fomenter par ces benefices temporels les tendres principes d'une telle quelle brute connoissance. . . . Et, de toutes les religions que Saint Paul trouva en credit à Athenes, celle qu'ils avoyent desdiée à une Divinité cachée et inconnue luy sembla la plus excusable.
>
> And of all the religions that St. Paul found in credit at Athens the one that they had dedicated to a hidden and unknown Diety seemed to him the most excusable.[23]

Montaigne then characterizes the views of some thirty ancient philosophers (including Plato and Aristotle) on the nature of the divinity, and refers to them as "the clatter of so many philosophical brains." The confusion, however, humbles and instructs him, and reminds him that "Reason does nothing but go astray . . . when it meddles with divine things" and that "when it strays however little from . . . the way traced and trodden by the church, immediately it is lost."[24] The greatness of God cannot be grasped by human understanding:

> . . . s'il s'est aucunement communiqué à toy, ce n'est pas pour . . . te donner le contrerolle de son pouvoir.
>
> . . . if he has communicated himself at all to you, it is not . . . to give you surveillance over his powers. . . . [25]
>
> . . . nos mouvements et nos mesures ne le touchent pas.
>
> . . . our movements and our measures do not touch him.[26]
>
> Les hommes, dict sainct Paul, sont devenus fols, cuidans estre sages; et ont mué la gloire de Dieu incorruptible en l'image de l'homme corruptible.
>
> "Men," says St. Paul, "professing themselves to be wise, became fools, and changed the glory of the incorruptible God into an image made like to corruptible man."[27]

Montaigne criticizes even popular Christian conceptions of God for constructing the deity on the basis of a relationship to themselves, quoting approvingly St. Augustine on the same point: *"In truth it is not God, whom they cannot conceive . . . not him but themselves whom they compare . . . with themselves. . . .* [28]

Montaigne also extends this criticism to ideas of God having carnal knowledge of women, and divinely sired virgin births. It is not clear whether by implication he means this criticism to extend to Catholic Christianity, but his conception of God as immutable and timeless would seem to imply that most of the biblical account must be metaphorical; yet it could also simply imply that Christian doctrines, insofar as they are logically and scientifically incredible, can be grasped only by the gift of faith. (More of this later.)

Montaigne next asks whether dogmatic philosophy (which he names "sophisticated poetry") has any more clarity in its knowledge of human or natural things than in its knowledge of divine things. His basic answer is negative, since all dogmatic systems are built on some first principles which are not susceptible of demonstration ("unless the Divinity has revealed them"), in spite of our elevated claims for human reason. This limit is more apparent in philosophy's confused attempts to understand, locate, and characterize the human soul. Montaigne characterizes a dozen of them, including those of Thales, Plato, Aristotle, and Chrysippus, and concludes that the various reasoned accounts of the soul must have been a form of amusement, for

> Ils ne veulent pas faire profession expresse d'ignorance et de l'imbecillité de la raison humaine, pour ne faire peur aux enfants; mais ils nous la descouvrent assez soubs l'apparence d'une science trouble et inconstante.
>
> *They do not want openly to profess ignorance and the imbecility of human reason, so as not to frighten the children, but they reveal it to us clearly enough under the guise of a muddled and inconsistent knowledge.*[29]

(In fact, so varied have been the faces of philosophy that even Montaigne's own unique imagination has found precedents with some ancient philosopher or another; hence he names himself "an unpremediated and accidental philosopher."[30]) Montaigne also observes in this discussion that philosophers have been powerless to *prove* the immortality of the soul by their own reason, another testament to the pride and vanity of human knowledge as reflected in the biblical account of the ancient tower of Babel:

> Tout ce que nous entreprenons sans son assistance, tout ce que nous voyons sans la lampe de sa grace, ce n'est que vanité et folie. . . . Quelque train que l'homme preigne de soy, Dieu permet qu'il arrive tousjours à cette mesme confusion. . . .
>
> All that we undertake without his assistance, all that we see without the lamp of his grace, is only vanity and folly. . . . *Whatever course man takes by himself, God allows him always to arrive at the same confusion.* . . .[31]
>
> . . . c'estoit vrayment bien raison que nous fussions tenus a Dieu seul . . . de la verité d'une si noble creance, puis que de sa seule liberalité nous recevons le fruit de l'immortalité. . . . car leçon n'est ce pas de nature et de nostre raison.
>
> . . . it was quite right that we should be beholden to God alone . . . for the truth of so noble a belief, *since from his liberality alone we receive the fruit of immortality* . . . for a lesson of nature and of our reason it is not.[32]

After a brief digression (for the one to whom the essay is addressed) on the necessity for bridling and keeping in tutelage most human minds, Montaigne returns to the theme of the weakness of human knowledge, this time through an exploration of the mutability of the knowing self. Many of his examples here are taken from his own introspective experience. Montaigne takes it as evidence of the lack of clarity in our "natural judgment" that there is "no proposition . . . which is not debated and controverted among us" and which our judgment can make another's judgment accept, "which is a sign that I have grasped it by some other means than by a natural power that is in me and in all men."[33]

Yet this confusion of our judgment is evident in more than the diversity of opinion which we encounter in the human race; it is evident in our own mutability, or at any rate, in Montaigne's own mutability, which frankly seems excessive, even if his dramatic hyberpole is taken into account:

> . . . combien de fois changeons nous nos fantasies? Ce que je tiens aujourd'huy et ce que je croy, je le tiens et le croy de toute ma croyance. . . . mais ne m'est il pas advenu, non une fois, mais . . . mille, et tous le jours, d'avoir ambrassé quelqu'autre chose a tout ces mesmes instrumens, en cette mesme condition, que depuis j'aye jugée fauce?

> How many times we change our notions! What I hold today and what I believe, I hold and believe it with all my belief. . . . *But has it not happened to me, not once, but . . . a thousand times, and every day, to have embraced with these same instruments, in this same condition, something else that I have since judged false?*[34]

He next says that "whatever we learn, we should always remember that it is man that gives and man that receives," and that only things which "come to us from heaven have . . . the right and authority for persuasion, alone the stamp of truth," and we do not "receive by our own means," unless God reforms us "by his particular and supernatural grace and favor."[35] (It is not entirely clear here whether Montaigne is saying that in the latter, divinely aided case what is involved is no longer man giving and receiving to man, or whether Montaigne is engaging in Pyrrhonian juxtaposition of contrarieties, though I think the former.)

Montaigne continues to counsel caution in trusting our judgment, since it is often contradictory and deceived, and emphasizes his point by returning to the theme of the vanity, weakness, and mutability which he finds in his own self. As if to anticipate at this point the reader's reactions to Montaigne's writing, he confronts us with its mercurial character:

> En mes escris mesmes je ne retrouve pas tousjours l'air de ma premiere imagination: je ne sçay ce que j'ay voulu dire . . . souvent à corriger et ye mettre un nouveau sens, pour avoir perdu le premier, qui valloit mieux. Je ne fay qu'aller et venir. . . .
>
> Even in my own writings I do not always find again the sense of my first thought; *I do not know what I meant to say,* and often I get burned by correcting and putting in a new meaning because I have lost the first one, which was better . . . *my judgment does not always go forward; it floats; it strays. . . .*[36]

Lest the reader lose interest in following his thoughts at this point, Montaigne observes that men (including philosophers) sometimes produce their greatest efforts when "out of their minds and frenzied" they approach divinity: "We improve by the privation and deadening of our reason," for while the spirit is within man, it reasons within shadows and ignorance. Montaigne also informs us that from the mutability and mobility within himself, he has accidentally engendered a "certain constancy of opinions" and has "scarcely altered" his "original and natural ones." So, by implication, although he is very mutable "within himself," he sees certain patterns in his reactions which reveal his original uniqueness to himself, and which can be generalized about. In particular, to prevent himself "from rolling about incessantly," among various philosophic, scientific, and religious viewpoints, he has kept himself intact "in the ancient beliefs of our religion."[37]

Again, the reason for this choice (not to choose anew) seems to be the weakness of human reason. Montaigne states a series of Pyrrhonian-like observations on law and religion, the upshot of which appears to be that his own religion is the true religion and different from all previous religions, but by logical implication could also imply that his religion too is simply a human creation if taken merely on grounds of logic. Here are the pertinent parts of this passage of Montaigne's argument. If we try to rule our conduct through our own knowledge, we are led into confusion from the standpoint of universal truth, for to obey the laws of one's own country (as philosophers like Socrates counsel with the claim of divine guidance) is to have as our duty "no rule but an accidental one." For laws are subject to constant agitation and are but the "undulating sea of opinions of a people or a prince," differing from country to country: "What of a truth that is bounded by these mountains and is falsehood to the world that lives beyond?"[38] And Montaigne doubts the existence of any natural or universally approved law among humankind. The counsel of the ancient god Apollo, that for each man the true cult was that of the location he was in, was testimony to the inability of human knowledge to know the divine, a folly from which are "we" not rescued, Montaigne asks, by our sovereign creator who bases our belief "on the eternal foundation of his holy word!"[39]

The next stage in Montaigne's questioning of the adequacy of human knowledge is his consideration of the claim (by the Epicureans, for example) that knowledge of things and pleasure both reside in our senses. He starts with his own conclusion that in our senses "lies the greatest foundation and proof of our ignorance." Interestingly, in this section of the argument, there is little juxtaposition of contrary opinions—almost all of the argument is directed toward subverting the testimony of our senses. (One witty exception is Montaigne's *juxtaposing* of the contrary views of the Epicureans that if the testimony of the senses is false, there is no knowledge possible, and the Stoic view that the testimony of the senses is false, to conclude himself "at the expense of these two great dogmatic sects that there is no knowledge."[40])

Montaigne's observations on the senses include the following. Since we observe animals which live self-contained lives without all the senses we have (e.g., sight and hearing), and others which appear to have senses we do not (such as a cock knowing when to crow), perhaps there are senses we lack necessary to gain a complete and true picture of things:

> Nous avons formé une verité par la consultation et concurrence de nos cinq sens; mais à l'advanture falloit-il l'accord de huict ou de dix sens et . . . pour l'appercevoir certainement et en son essence.
>
> We have found a truth by the consultation and concurrence of our five senses; *but perhaps we needed the agreement of eight or ten senses—to perceive it certainly* and in its essence.[41]

He also observes that senses can give false testimony (e.g., the case of a mirage or of two objects in the distance which appear close but are far apart); that they can contradict one another (as, for example, between sight and touch); and that their testimony differs from individual to individual, and from individuals to animals (in which a faculty, such as sight or smell, may be far keener). He reasons that since the senses give uncertain and contradictory testimony, they cannot solve the problem of infinite regress in the case of conflicting claims between the senses and reason over the validity of our apprehension of appearances:

> Pour juger des apparences que nous recevons des subjects, il nous faudroit un instrument judicatoire; pour verifier cet instrument, il nous y faut de la demonstration; pour verifier la demonstration, un instrument: nous violà au rouet. Puis que les sens ne peuvent arrester nostre dispute, estans pleins eux-mesmes d'incertitude, il faut que ce soit la raison; aucune raison ne s'establira sans une autre raison: nous voylà à reculons jusques à l'infiny.

> To judge the appearance that we receive of objects, we would need a judicatory instrument; to verify this instrument, we need a demonstration; to verify the demonstration, an instrument: *there we are in a circle*. Since the senses cannot decide our dispute, being full of uncertainty, it must be reason. No reason can be established without another reason: *there we go retreating back to infinity*.[42]

In addition, if someone should want to judge entirely by appearances anyway, there is still a problem, for appearances often contradict one another. How shall we decide which select appearances should rule others, since this claim requires a justification, and so on? From this point, Montaigne launches into his final arguments to suggest that nothing in the world of flux can be known by anything else in the world of flux, nor can changing human beings know unchanging God. Let us follow this last portion of the essay, which relies heavily on a moral essay by Plutarch (and has the feeling of having been written for another occasion and attached as the conclusion of "The Apology").

Montaigne's point here, reminiscent of ancient Greek ontological dualism, is that human beings and their reason can "have no communication with being" because human beings are immersed in the realm of becoming, of perpetual change from birth to death, and being is unchanging. Human reason is "baffled" by anything really stable, and unable to apprehend it. *There "is nothing" in the human world "that abides and is always the same."*[43] What then "really is"? Only God is eternal and has being:

> Ce qui est eternel, c'est à dire qui n'a jamais eu de naissance, ny n'aura jamais fin; à qui le temps n'apporte jamais aucune mutation.... Parquoy il faut conclurre que Dieu seul est, non poinct selon aucune mesure du temps, mais selon une eternité immuable et immobile....

Montaigne's Religious Views • 75

> That which is eternal: that is to say, what never had birth, nor will ever have an end; to which time brings no change. . . . Wherefore we must conclude that *God alone is—not at all according to any measure of time, but according to an eternity immutable* and immobile. . . .[44]

And the only way man can raise himself above his mere humanity is through the gift of divine grace:

> Il s'eslevera si Dieu lui preste extraordinairement la main. . . . abandonnant et renonçant à ses propres moyens. . . . C'est à nostre foy Chrestienne, non à sa vertu Stoique, de pretendre à cette divine et miraculeuse metamorphose.
>
> *He will rise, if God by exception lends him a hand, . . . by abandoning and renouncing his own means.* . . . It is for our Christian faith, not for . . . stoical virtue, to aspire to that divine and miraculous metamorphosis.[45]

By way of making an assessment of Montaigne's religious views, especially based on this long essay we have just summarized, let us look first at the critique of it by Montaigne's near-contemporary, the Fideist thinker and writer Blaise Pascal (1623–1662). In my view Pascal is still one of Montaigne's most insightful religious critics, even if not always an entirely fair and discriminating one. Pascal's views come from a paragraph on Montaigne in the *Pensées* and a more extended critique of "The Apology" in a work based on Pascal's notes of a discussion with a Monsieur de Sacy at the Port Royal monastery.[46] The brunt of Pascal's critique is that Montaigne is a complete Pyrrhonist who doubts everything; that he is most useful in deflating the inflated and prideful claims of reason and least useful for souls with a leaning toward impiety and vice; and that generally the effect of his work is to lead toward laziness and apathy, toward the disorder introduced into the world by sin, and toward an indifferent attitude regarding salvation, devoid of fear and repentance. Here are some of Pascal's more interesting insights:

> . . . he says that without faith everything is uncertain, and considering how many there are searching for truth and goodness with no progress towards peace of mind that *we must leave that task to others; we must remain . . . at ease,* floating lightly over subjects . . . *taking truth and goodness at face value because they are so flimsy* that . . . they disappear between the fingers, leaving you empty handed.[47]

> So . . . he goes about his business like everyone else, and *everything they do in the belief they are following the path of true goodness, he does from another*

principle, which is that the similarities are equal on both sides; example and convenience are the balancing factors which motivate him . . . *the overriding rule for his actions being convenience and calm.*[48]

To restate Pascal's criticisms in different terms, he appears to be saying that Montaigne follows Pauline Christianity in its emphasis on our seeing now "through a glass darkly," but not in its rejection of pagan attempts at psychic harmony and contentment over spiritual insights gained in the perpetual struggle with human sin. Montaigne wants his Christian morality to be easy, convenient and more realistic about the appetites of the body, Pascal implies. In my view, these Pascalian observations are largely on the mark and would seem to follow from Montaigne's conception of a distant, immutable, and unchangeable God, unknowable by changeable human beings immersed in the passages of "becoming," except through the gift of his grace—a phrase Montaigne adds in an almost mechanical way, without any exploration of its infusion in performance of religious ritual or actions toward others. (Is this one reason why Pascal appears to accuse Montaigne of vanity?) These implications also suggest that for Montaigne religion may have been definitionally a public matter, a largely ritualistic and formal activity, a matter very much constitutive of social order. If this is correct, then Montaigne could consistently encourage self-exploration and individual judgment and choice in private life, without extending this encouragement into the realm of religious belief as did Protestantism. (Yet without condoning Protestantism, he could attempt to moderate vehemence against it on grounds of the weakness and fallibility of all human judgment, Catholicism included.)

Pascal's other claim, that Montaigne was a complete Pyrrhonist in universal doubt, seems less obvious, for we have seen Montaigne admit that he has accidentally evolved into certain constant views, such as the wrongness of cruelty and torture or the uncertainty of the evidence of the senses. More generally, it is clear that Montaigne does not simply follow Pyrrhonian advice to accept the world of appearances and live within it—he is drawn to find out the truth at least about himself.[49] (And Pascal does only *imply* that Montaigne performs religious rituals in an empty, mechanical way, that is, vainly and without the infusion of grace.) In any event, Pascal never explicitly accuses Montaigne of atheism or even agnosticism, the latter of which would seem a logical possibility if Montaigne were in universal doubt. (The latter claims come from different sources and are explored in the concluding bibliographic essay.)

What kind of sustainable generalizations about Montaigne's religious views are we entitled to, then, based on our reading and summary of the arguments of "The Apology"?[50] Although Montaigne was a Catholic layman who eschewed formal theology, he gives us his own implied synthesis of the tensions in his civilizational inheritance, Greco-Roman and Judeo-Christian—for example, that between a distant, unchanging God of pure thought and a willful creator who also bestows grace upon his creations; between reasoned belief and inherited revelation; between a loose pagan sexual morality and a more rigid one; and so on. Let us look at the identifiable parts of Montaigne's account and attempt a statement of the *implied* synthesis in it.

We are given a version of a Plutarchian account of a distant, timeless, unchanging God; of the paucity of human reason to understand itself, its relation to the world, or its relation to God; of human beings as *unified* amalgams of body and soul, attempting harmony among their various and other contradictory impulses, both appetitive and ratiocinative, a harmony impossible without the bestowal of God's grace; and of faith as primarily as matter of belief in a set of inherited, public religious practices, rather than an intense, inarticulable experience of God's revelation (as in the Fideist account). Montaigne's Roman pragmatism combines these parts in a synthesis with no fewer tensions than has the synthesis of St. Thomas Aquinas. Montaigne employs ancient skeptical arguments against ancient rationalist arguments to support his view of the most humble capacities of human reason, a reason which still, however, drives him to give as coherent an account as possible of his inherited and individual contradictions. This reduced reason's appreciation of its own limits, in turn, makes it especially aware of its need for the active intervention (through the gifts of grace and faith) of a changeless God in human history, whose presence is visible in an earthly church and its rituals and practices. And Montaigne's account of human beings as unified amalgams of body and soul (following the logical implication of the symbol of the Trinity) eschews both extreme appetitive denial as well as single-minded cultivation of the intellect. Appropriate living (a life of psychic repose) for such creaturely amalgams of faith, passion, and reason involves a realistic appraisal of their actual capacities and points, for the vast majority of human beings, in the direction of a life emphasizing the ritualistic aspects of all activity, both public and private. For, as we have seen in the preceding chapter, it is the ritualistic aspect of especially public activity which most lends itself to being done for its own sake and in the present moment.

CHAPTER IV

Montaigne's Political Views

Montaigne wrote the *Essais* during several decades of religious and civil turmoil and war, that is, during very politically and socially unstable times. How far this historical circumstance can go in explaining Montaigne's views on politics and the limits of political action I leave for the reader to decide. Nevertheless, we can observe that Montaigne's political teaching (and I think he has one which can be drawn out by implication) is relatively internally coherent and consistent with his moderate philosophic skepticism; and generally it aims to achieve civil stability and consistency with the establishment and security of a private realm of intellectual freedom. As one cannot fail to observe, there are both "conservative" and "liberal" features *(avant la lettre)* in Montaigne's political outlook. We can also observe before proceeding that Montaigne endorses no specific governmental forms, arrangements, or institutions and has no theory of individual rights. He does have a distinct view, however, about the importance of a private realm of the conscience; about its superiority to public life in a balanced, contented life; and about the general limits of all political action, given human nature and the centrality of self-interest and self-love in it.

Take first Montaigne's skepticism about the possibilities of broad, innovative, or revolutionary political action. Given the limits of what human beings can know, and the uncertainty and moral corruption inherent in the realm of politics, Montaigne generally believes it desirable to support whatever political system one is born to, or in which one finds oneself, and not only in revolutionary times. Here are some of his thoughts on this score:

Je suis desgousté de la nouvelleté, quelque visage qu'elle porte, et ay raison, car j'en ay veu des effets tres- dommageables.

I am disgusted with innovation, in whatever guise, and with good reason, for I have seen the very harmful effects of it.[1]

Ceux qui donnent le branle à un estat, sont volontiers les premiers absorbez en sa ruyne. Le fruict du trouble ne demeure guere à celuy qui l'a esmeu. . . .

Those who give the first shock to a state are apt to be the first ones swallowed up in its ruin. The fruits of the trouble rarely go to the one who has stirred it up. . . . [2]

Il y a grand à dire, entre la cause de celui qui suyt les formes et les loix de son pays, et celui qui entreprend de les regenter et changer . . . car qui se mesle de choisir et de changer, . . . et se doit faire fort de voir la faute de ce qu'il chasse, et le bien de ce qu'il introduit . . . me semblant tres-inique de vouloir sousmettre les constitutions et observances publiques . . . à l'instabilité d'une privée fantasie (la raison privée n'a qu'une jurisdiction privée). . . .

There is a great difference between the cause of the man who follows the forms and laws of his country and that of the one who undertakes to control and change them. . . . For whoever meddles with choosing and changing . . . must be very sure that he sees the weakness of what he is carting out and the goodness of what he is bringing in. . . . *For it seems to me very iniquitous to want to subject public . . . institutions and observances to the instability of a private fancy* (private reason has only a private jurisdiction). . . . [3]

The exception which Montaigne makes to these observations praising prejudice in support of existing laws is in times of extreme necessity, especially necessities created by violent innovations (e.g., Protestantism):

Si est-ce que la fortune, reservant tousjours son authorité au-dessus de nos discours, nous presente aucunefois la necessité si urgente, qu'il est besoing que les loix luy facent quelque place.

Yet it is true that Fortune, always reserving her authority above our reasonings, *sometimes presents us with such an urgent necessity that the laws must give some place to it.*[4]

In this same essay ("Of custom, and not easily changing an accepted law"), Montaigne also praises the Christian religion for its "recommendation of obedience and maintenance of the government." And although, characteristically,[5] he does not cite the salient scriptural support for this (the famous chapter 13 of St. Paul's epistle to the Romans on *not* resisting secular rulers), his reasoning for it has similiarities[6] to Augustine's recommendation to the poor and enslaved not to resist their rulers and masters, because the political realm is simply not that important, nor can one have sufficient control over its vicissitudes:

> ... que le sage doit au dedans retirer son ame de la presse, et la tenir en liberté et puissance de juger librement des choses; mais, quant au dehors, qu'il doit suivre entierement les façons et formes receues. La société publique n'a que faire de nos pensées; mais ... nos actions, ... il la faut préter et abandonner à son service et aux opinions communes....

> ... that the wise man should withdraw his soul within, out of the crowd, and keep it in freedom and power to judge things freely; *but as for externals, he should wholly follow the accepted fashions and forms.* Society in general can do without our thoughts; but ... our actions. ... we must lend and abandon to its service and to the common opinions....[7]

Montaigne's reasons for obeying law under most conditions are also consistent with his general advice on supporting existing orders and obeying existing laws. For him, the authority of law is self-grounding and derives neither from its rationality nor its propensity to cultivate virtue, nor its ability to provide justice; additionally, the origins of laws are better not pursued, since they are often sordid, and investigating origins detracts from the important and necessary mystery of their authority.

> Or les loix se maintiennent en credit, non par ce qu'elles sont justes, mais par ce qu'elles sont loix. C'est le fondement mystique de leur authorité; elles n'en ont poinct d'autre. Qui bien leur sert. Elles sont souvent faictes par des sots. ... Quiconque leur obeyt parce qu'elles sont justes, ne leur obeyt pas justement par où il doibt.

> Now laws remain in credit not because they are just, but because they are laws. That is the mystic foundation of their authority; they have no other. And this is a good thing for them. They are often made by fools. ... Whoever obeys them because they are just does not obey them for just the reason he should.[8]

Montaigne's view of governance and law, then, is that it properly exists to provide the peace and order necessary for private cultivation of the self, and that it is in the interest of all reflective rulers and ruled to come to this realization. To attempt more than this is folly based on unrealistic appraisals of the limits to human knowledge and practical action, especially the attempt politically to suppress the realm of the individual conscience and private individual intellectual discourse. Montaigne's reason for wanting to preserve a "private room" is for cultivation and realization of private "corners of the soul," for essaying oneself by experimentation, deliberation, judgment, and choice about properly private matters. Montaigne's ideas about self-exploration are uniquely his own and have affinities with modern individualism, a complex of ideas which are arguably at least a partial consequence of the influence of Montaigne's *Essais*.

Montaigne's reason for downplaying the importance of political life, especially at high levels, would seem to flow from observations he made as emissary, negotiator, and advisor to kings (Henry III and Henry IV) and as mayor of Bordeaux for two consecutive terms. Montaigne's view is that high politics inevitably at certain times requires one to dissemble, deceive, even act treacherously for the good of the whole; that *contra* Cicero, morality and political expediency are often at odds. (As we have seen, his views anticipate in a vague way Rousseau's idea that public life or life in society is a tissue of contradictions which pits us against ourselves and each other.) For this reason, Montaigne is inclined to avoid political life as much as possible, while still discharging his unavoidable civic duties toward others. Or, as he says, he performs his public professions in "the most private manner I can." Here are some of his observations in this connection.

> Le bien public requiert qu'on trahisse et qu'on mente et qu'on massacre; resignons cette commission à gens . . . plus souples.
>
> The public welfare requires that a man betray and lie and massacre; let us resign this commission to . . . suppler people.[9]
>
> . . . et ne hay pas seulement à piper, mais je hay aussi qu'on se pipe en moy. Je n'y veux pas seulement fournir de matiere et d'occasion.
>
> And not only do I hate to deceive, but I hate to see anyone deceived by me. I do not even want to furnish matter for occasion for deceiving.[10]
>
> Tendre negotiateur et novice, qui ayme mieux faillir à l'affaire qu'à moy!
>
> . . . myself . . . a tender and green negotiator, who would rather fail in my mission than fail to be true to myself.[11]

However, Montaigne does not find acceptable, even in times of civil war, simply remaining neutral or sitting on a fence. He supports what he takes to be the right cause moderately and without enthusiasm, in his case the Catholic cause and the French monarchy he was born to:

> Les loix m'ont osté de grand peine; elles m'ont choisy party . . . toute autre superiorité et obligation doibt estre relative à celle là et retrenchée.

> The laws have freed me from great anxiety; they have chosen me my party. . . . Any other superiority and obligation must be relative to that one, and restricted.[12]

> La cause generale et juste ne m'attache non plus que modéreement et sans fiévre. . . . Je suivray le bon party jusques au feu, mais exclusivement si je puis. Que Montaigne s'engouffre quant et la ruyne publique, si besoin est; mais, s'il n'est pas besoin, je sçauray bon gré à la fortune qu'il se sauve. . . .

> I am attached to the general and just cause only with moderation and without feverishness. . . . *I will follow the good side right to the fire, but not into it if I can help it.* Let Montaigne be engulfed in the public ruin, if need be; but if not I shall be grateful to fortune if it is saved. . . . [13]

One of the strong reasons for avoiding high political office, then, is that at some point individual morality and public necessity will inevitably diverge, and being true to his private self is of paramount importance for Montaigne, especially in the matter of keeping faith with friends.

> . . . j'estime tous les hommes mes compatriotes, et embrasse un Polonis comme un François, postposant cette lyaison nationale à l'universelle et commune. . . . Les amitiez pures de nostre acquest emportent ordinairement celles ausquelles la communication du climat ou du sang nous joignent.

> . . . I consider all men my compatriots, and embrace a Pole as I do a Frenchman, setting this national bond after the common and universal one. . . . *Friendships of our own acquisition usually surpass those to which community of climate or blood binds us.*[14]

> L'unique et principale amitié descoust toutes autres obligations.

> *A single dominant friendship dissolves all other obligations.*[15]

A concatenation of causes—the uncertainty of political "knowledge," the moral corruption of political life, the delights of private attachments—

push or nudge Montaigne away from Aristotelian and Ciceronian ideas about the centrality of politics and oratory in human fulfillment. Still, he sees that we are often called on to act in public ways and often have no defensible basis to refuse. This lends Montaigne a rather light-hearted attitude to political and social life, generally, to a view of public life as a series of roles to be played, as in a game or on the stage. Montaigne often uses the analogy of theater roles and gaming to approach the appropriate way to fulfill public obligations and some private ones:

> Il n'est rien si beau et legitime que de faire bien l'homme et deuëment. . . .
>
> There is nothing so beautiful and legitimate *as to play the man well and properly.* . . .[16]
>
> La plus part de nos vactions sont farcesques. . . . Il faut jouer deuement nostre rolle, mais comme rolle d'un personnage emprunté. Du masque et de l'apparence il n'en faut pas faire une essence réelle, ny de l'estranger le propre. . . . C'est assés de s'enfariner le visage, sans s'enfariner la poictrine. . . . Le Maire et Montaigne ont tousjours esté deux, d'une separation bien claire.
>
> Most of our occupations are low comedy. . . . *We must play our part duly, but as the part of a borrowed character. Of the mask and appearance we must not make a real essence,* nor what is foreign our own. . . . It is enough to make up our face, without making up our heart. . . . The mayor and Montaigne have always been two, with a very clear separation.[17]

This recurrent theme in the *Essais* about discerning wisely and playing one's part appropriately and well would seem to follow from Montaigne's appraisal of the limits of human knowledge and action and from his estimation of the moral corruption inherent in high politics. Montaigne resists complete withdrawal, recognizing that we are made to act, but encourages action *with* moderation and without the kind of enthusiasm which can lead to psychic imbalance and political and religious fanaticism. In this he can be seen to diverge from and repudiate the ancient Roman aristocratic political *ethos* and its implicit view that the public mask was everything,[18] and that the kinds of private considerations (which are Montaigne's subject matter) were inconsequential. But the reasons for this are more than merely moral; they have to do as well with Montaigne's estimation of the path to human contentment, which involves (though never entirely consistently so) the attempt to avoid using anything merely as the means to an end and whenever possible to perform actions for their own sake and enjoyment. We have developed this theme elsewhere, but in passing we may note that it is consistent with Montaigne's taste for the ritualistic aspects of life, rituals being human practices in which it is supremely appropriate to speak and act for its own sake, to immerse oneself completely in the present moment.

Montaigne's appreciation of the limits of political action is also consistent with his moderate philosophic skepticism in ways it is politically illuminating to note. We have seen that Montaigne thinks he has made a firm case (in "The Apology for Raymond Sebond") for the view that human beings are incapable of certain knowledge about either themselves or the world, because both are in a state of constant flux. Montaigne even doubts his ability to know himself except as a passage from one state to another (though this never stops him from trying in the *Essais*). This insight appears to have led him, as it did the ancient Skeptics, to value the world of established customs, practices, and political religious institutions as the only reliable source of human stability:

> Or de la cognoissance de cette mienne volubilité j'ay par accident engendré en moy quelque constance d'opinions, et n'ay guiere alteré les miennes premiers et naturelles. . . . je ne change pas aisément, de peur que j'ay de perdre au change. . . . Ainsi me suis-je, par la grace de Dieu, conservé entier, sans agitation et trouble de conscience, aux anciennes creances de nostre religion, au travers de tant de sectes et de divisions que nostre siecle a produittes.
>
> Now from the knowledge of this mobility of mine I have accidentally engendered in myself a certain constancy of opinions. . . . I do not change easily, for fear of losing in the change. . . . Thus, I have, by the grace of God, kept myself intact . . . in the ancient beliefs of our religion, in the midst of so many . . . divisions that our century has produced.[19]

As one commentator has explicitly stated on this point, "Montaigne needed a relatively stable public realm in order to anchor his unpredictable private self."[20] Perhaps so.

Another general connection between Montaigne's skepticism and political action and culture concerns its implications for what we now call individualism. To what extent is Montaigne's cultivation of individual self-exploration a consequence of his skepticism about the limits of human knowledge and his dramatic characterization of the human situation as a series of experiments in honing and refining our judgment under conditions of uncertainty? We can observe here that insofar as Montaigne accepts the arguments of Pyrrhonian skepticism that we can never through knowledge penetrate to a reality beyond the realm of appearances (and Montaigne certainly makes no attempt at such a penetration in the *Essais*), he is led to the importance of individual perspective on what is appearing at any moment in a way that naive philosophic realism or modern science, for example, are not. By implication, the collection of various individual perspectives on what is appearing is what makes up the (human) world. Montaigne's emphasis, then, on the importance of individual self-discovery and choice, in at least the private realm, does flow from his skeptical attitudes, not so much as a moral matter as from the impulse to discover the truth about at least the phenomenological structure of human reality and reality generally. (And this is so, even were he to come to the more "objective" view that under similar conditions human beings perceive the same appearances, which he does not.)

Montaigne's skepticism about the capacities of human knowledge can also explain the importance for him of the separation of the public and private realms and the cultivation and protection of the latter. For the "skeptical moment" in which we doubt our own conclusions and remain open to the truth of new and diverse human possibilities is most appropriate and prudent in a private realm. Such openness in public matters would threaten public order and impede the capacity for public action by impeding the capacity to act at all.

We can also observe two features of Montaigne's thought which have been historically characteristic of democratic culture, generally, and which are not directly connected to Montaigne's skepticism about human knowledge. (Though, by *no* means do they suggest Montaigne would have supported liberal democratic governance in sixteenth-century France.[21]) For one thing, Montaigne has an egalitarian side to him, at least in a grand cosmic sense, which sees that each individual contains the whole of the human possibility within him and which is prepared on occasion to assert that we are all part of the "common herd":

> Je propose une vie basse et sans lustre, c'est tout un. On attache aussi bien toute la philosophie morale à une vie populaire et privée que à une vie de plus riche estoffe: chaque homme porte la forme entiere de l'humaine condition.
>
> I set forth a humble and inglorious life; that does not matter. You can tie up all moral philosophy with a common and private life just as well as with a life of richer stuff. *Each man keeps the entire form of man's estate.*[22]

Je suis desgousté de maistrise et active et passive. . . . La superiorité et inferiorité, . . . sont obligées à une naturelle envie et contestation; il faut qu'elles s'entrepillent perpetuellement. Je ne crois ny l'une ny l'autre des droicts de sa compaigne: laissons en dire à la raison. . . .

I have a distaste for mastery, both active and passive . . . superiority and inferiority of position, mastery and subjection, are forced into a natural envy and contention; they must pillage one another perpetually. I do not believe either one about the rights of the other; let us give the floor to reason. . . .[23]

Another feature of Montaigne's outlook which may be considered democratic (certainly by the Platonic and Tocquevillean traditions) is his emphasis on sensual and bodily functions and satisfactions and his aggressive insistence on making them "public" by describing aspects of his bodily (and sexual) organs, even his sexual experience (which even now seems in bad taste, or, at least, intentionally provocative). Here are his stated reasons for these exhibitions:

En faveur des Huguenots, qui accusent nostre confession privée . . . je me confesse en publicq. . . . Je suis affamé de me faire connoistre; et ne me chaut à combien, pourveu que ce soit veritablement. . . .

In honor of the Huguenots, who condemn our private confession, . . . *I confess myself in public.* . . . I am hungry to make myself known, and I care not to how many, provided it be truly.[24]

Chacune de mes pieces me faict esgalement moy que toute autre. Et nulle autre ne me faict plus proprement homme que cette cy. Je dois au publiq universellement mon pourtrait . . . desdeignant . . . ces petites regles feintes, usuelles, provinciales. . . .

Each one of my parts makes me myself just as much as every other one. And no other makes me more properly a man than this one. *I owe a complete portrait of myself to the public . . . distaining . . . these petty, feigned, customary, provincial rules.* . . .[25]

J'ayme la modestie; et n'est par jugement que j'ay choisi cette sorte de parler scandaleux: c'est Nature qui l'a choisi pour moy. Je ne le loue . . . mais je l'excuse. . . .

I like modesty, and it is not by judgment that I have chosen *this scandalous way of speaking; it is nature that has chosen it for me.* I do not commend it . . . but I excuse it.[26]

> Pouvons nous pas dire qu'il n'y a rien en nous, pendant cette prison terrestre, purement ny corporel ny spirituel, et que injurieusement nous dessirons un homme tout vif....
>
> May we not say that *there is nothing in us during this earthly imprisonment that is purely either corporeal or spiritual, and that we do wrong to tear apart a living man.* ...[27]
>
> Moy ... hay cette inhumaine sapience qui nous veut rendre desdaigneux et ennemis de la culture du corps.
>
> *I ... hate that in human wisdom that would make us disdainful enemies of the cultivation of the body.*[28]

On this last point, I believe it is not inaccurate to say that in an attempt to re-right the balance between the corporeal and the spiritual in his own civilization, Montaigne employed rhetorical exaggerations enhancing the cultivation of the bodily associated with older or "mature" democratic cultures. And although it is difficult to demonstrate this kind of thing, it is certainly possible that Montaigne's confessions on this score had a cumulative effect over time on European attitudes toward literary and social treatment of bodily and sexual matters.

We can also discern some of Montaigne's general political viewpoint in his criticism of the cruel and exploitative Spanish colonial project and its conquest of Mexico and Peru and in his criticism of the arrogance of "civilized" Europe in failing to appreciate the purity, simplicity, and happiness of peoples closer to "nature." Here are some of Montaigne's observations on this score from the essays "Of cannibals" and "Of coaches," observations which develop classic pastoral themes later elaborated at great length by Rousseau:[29]

> Ces nations me semblent ... pour avoir receu fort peu de façon de l'esprit humain, et estre encore fort voisines de leur naifveté originelle. Les loix naturelles leur commandent encores, fort peu abastardies par les nostres; ... une nayfveté si pure et simple....
>
> *These nations, then, ... have been fashioned very little by the human mind, and are still very close to their original naturalness.* The laws of nature still rule them, very little corrupted by ours. ... *a naturalness so pure and simple.* ...[30]
>
> Nostre monde vient d'en trouver un autre. ... Bien crains-je que nous aurons bien fort hasté sa declinaison et sa ruyne par nostre contagion, et que nous luy aurons bien cher vendu nos opinions et nos arts.

> *Our world has just discovered another world. . . . I am much afraid that we shall have greatly hastened the decline and ruin of this world by our contagion,* that we will have sold it our opinions and our arts very dear.[31]

These criticisms of European colonialism are consistent with Montaigne's consistent aversion to complicated instrumental projects as the important activities in life; with his preference for activity done for its own sake, a tendency more evident in simpler, less "civilized" societies; and with his general aversion to cruelty of any sort.

Before leaving the subject of Montaigne's political views, let us recap. We see in this connection the following assessments and preferences in Montaigne's *Essais:* the paucity of human intellect to know the truth about anything, including itself; hence the importance by default of relying for guidance on inherited customs, institutions, and practices and on God's grace; a preference for activity done for its own sake and in the present moment over instrumental activity, hence for private activity over public activity; a recognition, nevertheless, of the importance of meeting civic obligations, dutifully though not enthusiastically; a view of law and government as deriving their authority and legitimacy from the mystery of their antiquity, not from their ability to provide justice; a view of religion as primarily a matter of public ritual rather than individual conscience; a preference for openness and transparency in all dealings; the importance of both bodily and spiritual satisfactions; a strong aversion to cruelty; a penchant for cultivation of individual uniqueness and diversity; a willingness to have a public effect if he could do so without betraying his own "ruling form"; and a preference for cheerful repose over fame, status, or power. All of these were more or less coherently combined in the person of Michel de Montaigne—a social, political, and religious conservative who also held certain ideas which would appeal to the subsequent liberal and democratic movement, and arguably influenced it; and who cultivated in private his own individuality in a monarchic system in some ways more tolerant of individual diversity (as Montesquieu and Tocqueville foresaw[32]) than would be those subsequent majoritarian political and social movements.

CHAPTER V

Bibliographic Essay

The commentary on and critique of Montaigne's *Essais* over the past four centuries are vast and still proliferating yearly. This chapter concentrates on summary and commentary of secondary literature on Montaigne from philosophical, political, and religious perspectives primarily, referring the general reader to other more specialized bibliographic essays, especially ones from more literary (including "postmodernist") perspectives and ones available only in French or languages other than English. It addresses works which are either relevant in their focus to our characterization of Montaigne's "art of living" or are simply compelling (not necessarily persuasive) or useful from philosophical, political, ethical, and religious perspectives.

A sound and useful work on Montaigne's near-contemporary influence and reception is still Alan Boase, *The Fortunes of Montaigne: A History of the Essays in France, 1580–1669*.[1] (The original 1935 edition was reprinted in 1970 and is available in many university libraries.) Generally useful chapters include those on Montaigne's early contemporary critics, on Marie de Gournay (Montaigne's acolyte), and on Pierre Charron, Descartes, La Rochefoucauld, Pascal, Moliére, and La Fontaine, among others. Some of Boase's introductory remarks characterizing Montaigne's outlook are still worth summarizing for our purposes.

Boase holds to a "developmentalist" view of Montaigne during the writing of the *Essais* (much of it based on the work of the French Montaigne scholar Pierre Villey), that is, that he passed through an initial *Stoic* period, to a *skeptical*,[2] *Fideist*[3] period during the writing of the long essay "Apology for Raymond Sebond," brought on by a reading of Sextus Empiricus, and on to a more Epicurean[4] period finally, wanting virtue to be easy, not conflictual. Here are some representative assertions from this argument:

> *Some such statement might serve as a picture of Montaigne's opinions round the year 1574 . . .*[5]

> As for *constance*, this has a double sense in the essays. It sometimes means endurance, but it more often means consistency. . . . *To possess his soul in peace and quiet . . . it is necessary for him to teach himself to be brave and happy in spite of possible misfortunes. . . . It is impossible to aspire to this self-possession except by consistency . . . yet there is nothing so astonishing in life as its variety. . . .*[6]

> *Then came the so-called skeptical crisis. . . . A realization of the interdependence of contraries,* an antinomianism and relativism, *was forced on him by reading of Sextus Empiricus and his preoccupation with the skepticism he was using to defend religion. . . . This relativism encouraged at the same time his interest in introspection.*[7]

> *In his insistence on harmony, not conflict, and on the importance of individual nature, Montaigne revived two of the most important ideas of Epicurus, but the twist he gives them is an unholy personal one.*[8]

> *To sum up, Montaigne absorbs ethics into a kind of general aesthetic of life. . . . Art is in its essence a heightening of consciousness and a harmonizing of contrary impulses. Order and consistency are the means to this end. This fittingness, this being adapted to oneself and one's circumstances, in which the concept of duty loses itself. . . .*[9]

Needless to say, our chapter on Montaigne's art of living attempted a synthesis of his various ideas around the idea of doing things for their own sake, insofar as possible, rather than choosing the developmentalist approach as a more philosophically enlightening approach to consistency and coherence in the *Essais*.

Another well-known "developmentalist" account of Montaigne's *Essais*, and of himself, is to be found in Donald M. Frame, *Montaigne: A Biography*.[10] Frame sees Montaigne moving from a concern with mastering fear of death to an embracing of life, from an individualistic concern with learning to belong to oneself to a concern for human solidarity, from Christian ethics to a humanist ethics, and from a tentative style to a bolder, assertive one. Here are some representative assertions:

> *Over his last twenty years . . . Montaigne's writings show a number of striking modifications. . . . He first calls death the goal of life and philosophy a learning to die; later it is philosophy that teaches us to live,* and death is the end but not the goal of life. . . . After urging a tense defense against the ills of life, he later says we do better to relax. . . . *After seeing little but diversity in man and life, he comes to see unity as well.*[11]

> *The extreme withdrawal* expressed in his early remark "The greatest thing in the world is to know how to belong to onself," though not contradicted, is not reaffirmed; and one of the final additions tends to modify it: "He who lives not at all unto others, hardly lives unto himself."[12]

Obviously, in the view I have presented regarding Montaigne's general orientation to living, these "changes" may all be viewed as differences in emphasis and context more satisfactorily than as marks of transformation in Montaigne. For instance, learning how to belong to oneself can certainly accommodate the importance of connections with others; there are moods and seasons when it is appropriate to "tense oneself" and others to relax; Montaigne surely did not come to appreciate unity as well as diversity only after he aged and evolved, and so on.

A full-length twentieth-century study of the *Essais*, which is still profitably read in graduate schools and which does *not* take an evolutionary or developmentalist approach, is *Montaigne* by Hugo Friedrich (originally published in German in 1949). This learned and erudite book in the old style (before the contemporary era of fragmented academic specialization) attempts to explain Montaigne by situating him intellectually in the late Renaissance and exploring his links to its concerns (and its fascination with ancient authors). There is virtually no issue of contemporary specialization on which one cannot find some interesting observations in Friedrich's book. His general themes are that (1) Montaigne from the beginning identifies "the predominant moral theme of the *Essais*, namely the question of whether one can come to an understanding of concrete changeable man with general, rigid maxims";[13] and that (2) Montaigne throughout individual essays and the essays as a whole pursues an analytic strategy which moves from "man abased" to "man affirmed" to a simple phenomenological investigation of what is immediately at hand, including the contents of his own self at the moment. In addition to these general themes, however, are scores of insightful and sound observations eloquently expressed in Friedrich's work. Here are several representative ones. First, on the differences between Montaigne's subjectivity and the willful subjectivity of the Baconian and Cartesian project to subdue and master nature:

> ... *while the science of his time,* working its transition to technology and rational organization, is *still calling upon the biblical core of this idea:* "Fill the earth and subdue it, and have dominion. . . . " Montaigne's man—who never aspires to be more than he, Montaigne, himself is—*does not feel himself to be the lord of nature, but rather its protégée* . . . he does not want the will to power, but rather . . . to powerlessness.[14]

> ... *just before the rational subjectivity of the modern scientific approach steps into technical mastery of the world,* here in Montaigne that subjectivity . . . of quite a different order . . . it is also secular, but closer . . . to piety . . . which, the more "subjective" it becomes, the more carefully *it limits itself to listening and obeying.*[15]

And on the insight implicit in Montaigne's skeptical stance, an insight compatible with our characterization of delight in the present moment:

> *Skepticism* is unassumingness. It *tones man down and yet in the abasement of his place in the world it opens his eye to the miracle of the world,* pregnant with inexhaustibility—and the miracle of himself. . . .[16]

> *The miracles do* not just *begin* with the supernatural miracle, but rather *with the ordinary, customary thing, the wonder of which is veiled by its habitual nature.*[17]

And, finally, some observations on similarities between Montaigne and Erasmus, regarding the importance of human folly and illusion:

> *The two men* . . . have in common the fact that they compensate for the concept of the objective triviality of the totality of life with the escape of subjective delusion . . . *they shelter man in a wisdom which lies beyond the inconsequential contrast of reason and irrationality.* Both also have in common the fact that they *praise illusion as the mover of the human soul which brings happiness* . . . whether . . . in the simplicity of fools or in the vision of believers, or in the poets' prowess . . .[18]

Two commentators who give insightful analyses of the *Essais* from a philosophic perspective (versus intellectual history or literary criticism) are Tzvetan Todorov and Ann Hartle. Montaigne is one of the central authors analyzed in Todorov's *Imperfect Garden: The Legacy of Humanism* and the main subject of Hartle's *Michel de Montaigne: Accidental Philosopher.*[19]

Todorov sees Montaigne as breaking new ground in the humanist tradition[20] in his emphasis on himself for his own sake and, by implication, on the individual person for its own sake. More important for our purposes, however, Todorov is the only other commentator (except perhaps, obliquely, Michael Oakeshott[21]) who fixes on Montaigne's insight about doing things for their own sake in the present moment. Todorov sees Montaigne as coming out of the skeptical nominalist tradition of William of Occam (that nothing exists but instantaneous states and individual entities, that all universals are merely names) and, in effect, illustrating this nominalist insight in all sorts of mundane reflections. (Todorov also notes the influence of Horace and Seneca in Montaigne's orientation toward present delight.) Here are some of Todorov's observations, which support our characterizations of Montaigne's "art of living":

> The way of wisdom, in Montaigne, is plotted without any specific reference to others . . . simply to be here. *Here, the goal of the wise life, we might say, is to erase the difference between ends and means, to find the meaning of human actions in those actions themselves.*[22]

> Human life unfolds in time; *to renounce seeking an external purpose leads to an acceptance of living in the present.* Montaigne learned from Seneca and Horace that *those who endlessly project themselves into the future are condemned to perpetual frustration,* while those who know how to live in the present are blessed.[23]

> Certain actions . . . find their end outside themselves, but life has no purpose but itself. . . . 'The practice of everyday life should be an aim until itself.'[24]

Ann Hartle's work takes Montaigne seriously as a philosopher, that is, someone interested in penetrating as deeply as can be sustained into the structure of reality. Thus she does not see Montaigne as a Skeptic, though he obviously has skeptical moods (which only serve to make him more open to the truth). Hartle's reconstruction of Montaigne's implicit synthesis of pagan and Christian cosmological and ontological themes has him an "accidental philosopher," a phrase she employs to describe the limited role of human intellect immersed in the time-stream of a contingent or created universe. Her account of Montaigne's implied philosophic outlook is frankly reminiscent of Vico's account of the wisdom of the ancient Romans and Hume's account of the relationship between philosophy and morality generally—that there is a pre-reflective correspondence or unity between thought and being, and that the proper role of reflective thought is to penetrate to the insight in received, common, and pre-reflective practices and opinions, not to transcend or displace them as in the classic Rationalist tradition. Hartle says that Montaigne does this through a recurring approach she calls the "circular dialectic," which begins from Montaigne's received opinions only to return to those in a sense of wonder at the familiar, wonder at the creation of a world which might not have been or had no necessity to be. Hartle's "wonder at the familiar" has obvious similarities to the state of mind we have been describing by the phrase "delight in the present moment" and is made possible by the Christian rejection of classical ontological dualism and its view that the material, everyday world is fatally flawed.

The literature on Montaigne's religious views is vast, varied, and ranges from the view that he was a complete atheist intending to subvert religion (e.g., that of André Gide),[25] to the intermediate view that he professed Catholicism merely in order not to undermine the socially salutary views of ordinary believers,[26] to the view that he was a Skeptic-Fideist and sincere, practicing Catholic,[27] with variations of these main interpretations in between. If Montaigne's religious views were completely hidden, then this kind of debate would be completely superfluous, but if they were only veiled and implied, as some interpreters believe, then argument over which are Montaigne's real views can take place (and also create a little academic cottage industry of interpretation). By way of conveying some of the issues involved here, much of it centering on interpretation of the very long essay "Apology for Raymond Sebond," let us look at two more unusual arguments from the more recent literature in English (both of which cite important French secondary literature on this question), those of Ann Hartle and of Alan Levine.

Ann Hartle's views are laid out in several articles, in particular "The Dialectic of Faith and Reason in *The Essays of Montaigne.*"[28] Hartle, in a carefully reasoned argument, rejects the views of both atheism and skeptical Fideism and argues that what Montaigne defends in the "Apology" is "a *transformed version* of Sebond's fundamental thesis of the harmony of faith and reason, for example, *the harmony of examined faith and reformed reason.*"[29] Let us follow some of her reasoning. She notes persuasively in rejecting the claim of hidden atheism that a strong reason why many readers are reluctant to accept the view that Montaigne is lying, even for socially salutary reasons, is that it would constitute a complete betrayal of the bond Montaigne attempts to establish with the reader:

> What is offered to us in the *Essays* is not a mere verbal puzzle but the man himself and a man of a certain character, a man for whom truth is a moral imperative.[30]

(Needless to say, the atheistic interpretation would also constitute a direct repudiation of our characterization of Montaigne's art of living in the present moment over engaging in complex plans full of instrumentality and would thus constitute as well a denial of his entire *Weltanschauung*.) She also rejects the view that Montaigne is a Skeptic-Fideist for whom faith is entirely private and inarticulate, for it "amounts to a frustration of the natural desire to think honestly about one's life" as well as "to a condition of conflict within the self that is not at all evident in the *Essays*." She proceeds to explain in what way the "Apology" modifies Montaigne's inherited ideas on both reason and faith in order to conjoin them in a sustainable dialectic, rather than side exclusively with either of the two objections to Sebond which Montaigne identifies, the Fideist and the rationalist.

In brief, Hartle's view of Montaigne's implied meaning in the "Apology" is that there can be a harmony of faith and reason (and hence a defense of Sebond's general intent) only when human reason is brought down from its arrogant heights and shown that it is not the universal, autonomous, public form of communication it purports to be; and faith ceases to mean a private inarticulate experience of particular divine inspiration and comes to mean a common inherited belief passed and maintained by the church of Rome, that "great common way":

> *For Montaigne, the common bond among men is not be found in autonomous reason but in "the church"* ... *the truths of faith are common to the lowliest village woman and the greatest theologian.*[31]

In this argument, Hartle does not take a stance on whether Catholic Christianity as a system of inherited and institutionalized beliefs has a supernatural basis and priority for Montaigne among other established religions on earth, such as Islam and Hinduism. She stops short of affirming with Frieda Brown that the Catholic religion was an exception to Montaigne's account of the relativity of religious beliefs:

The same conviction was at the root of his skepticism and led him to doubt everything but the Catholic religion which he believed God had lodged in us "sur l'eternelle base de sa saincte parole."[32]

Brown's view is also supported by Catherine Demure in an article originally in French[33] on the paradox of the "Apology"—that Montaigne implies theology is both impossible yet necessary as a practical solution for a personal relationship with a distant, abstract God. Demure argues that Montaigne alters the object of "theology" in the "Apology" *from* the futile attempt to *know* God, *to* "a simple account . . . of the possibility of the divine in the world" as manifested especially in church dogma. Even this reduced theology, however, is beyond human rational capacity, except for the miraculous intervention of God's grace:

> . . . if God by exception lends him a hand; he will rise by abandoning and renouncing his own means, and letting himself be raised and uplifted by purely celestial means. (F437)[34]

For a recent, reasoned account which interprets Montaigne's support of religion solely for its utility, let us look at the relevant arguments of Alan Levine's *Sensual Philosophy*.[35] Drawing largely on assertions in the "Apology," Levine makes the following arguments, among others:

> Moreover despite numerous references to God, *Montaigne never says that he believes in a God*. . . . *We are not created in God's image, he argues, but create God in our own*. . . . To be useful in inspiring different peoples, God has been given a body 'as necessity required' (II, 12, 381). . . .[36]

> . . . *the conception of God that he describes as the 'most excusable' is more Greek (philosophic not Homeric) than Jewish or Christian* (II, 12, 280) . . . Montaigne . . . advises us not to concern ourself with thoughts of an afterlife. He dismisses the Garden of Eden version of natural man, the notion of a virgin birth (II, 12, 397), the doctrine of transubstantiation. . . . Montaigne further argues that God cannot be understood in human terms such as justice or goodness.[37]

Although Levine casts as certain some opinions which are arguably more tentative and exploratory on Montaigne's part, his points are useful (in my view) not in showing that Montaigne viewed religion solely in utilitarian terms, but rather in fleshing out Montaigne's peculiar synthesis of Greek and pagan ideas about God and morality with Judeo-Christian ones.

It is certainly true that Montaigne's God as described at the close of the "Apology" is a distant, unchanging Platonic-like God who does not concern himself with earthly events in the way of the New Testament God who sees "every sparrow that falls." It is also true that Montaigne does not encourage preoccupation with an afterlife, for as we have seen, that would be to turn daily living into the alienated, instrumental pursuit of a future imagined condition. It is also certainly true that Montaigne is not especially concerned with Christian sexual morality (although he reaches his arguments about the importance of an integration of body and soul via Augustinian reflections on the unity of the human personality as an analogue of the Trinity). And it is also true that he is impressed with the diversity of the world's religious interpretations of God's form and essence, even though he appears to privilege among religions the Roman Catholic, owing to its receipt of the gift of divine grace. All of these considerations, however, arguably point away from Levine's attributions of utilitarianism in Montaigne's view of religion and toward the problems and tensions in his particular synthesis of Judea, Athens, and Rome, no fewer than in the Aquinian synthesis (which Luther referred to as "the Aristotelian Church").

Readers interested in making a judgment on the importance of the practice of religion in the historic Montaigne's daily life might look at the obscure but informative little book by Malcolm Smith, *Montaigne and the Roman Censors*.[38] This book draws on Montaigne's travel journals, the *Essais*, and Montaignian and historical secondary literature to show how seriously and in what ways Montaigne responded to the various criticisms of the *Essais* by the papal censors during his travels in Italy—for example, his use of the word "fortune," his criticism of cruel punishments, his admonition of purity of conscience in prayer, his view of the proper education for children, and so on. Smith shows how important a part of Montaigne's life was the performance of Catholic rituals, as well as ways in which the papal censors' criticisms spurred Montaigne to amplify and modify his views on the subjects criticized. Smith also makes some interesting conjectures about how Montaigne was able to combine his skepticism, his belief in the free play of private inquiry, and his deference to the authority of church doctrine:

> . . . in Montaigne's view, intellectual freedom is the greatest friend of religious authority. *Intellectual freedom* . . . *brings the intellect up against its own limitations and thereby engenders receptiveness to divine authority* . . . and . . . to acknowledge our need for authoritative enlightenment from a higher source.[39]

We have seen him insist in Prayers that his is a human book, not a theological one. He would not have thought it right for a Roman Catholic layman to write professedly and in theological language about the "spiritual" life. . . . *Thus, those writers on Montaigne who infer from the paucity of reference in the Essays to his religious practice that Montaigne's practice was meagre are misunderstanding the nature of his book.* They are also overlooking . . . from the diary . . . that (for example) Montaigne frequently attended mass on weekdays, and maybe every day.[40]

Concerning Montaigne's political intentions in the *Essais*, there is less controversy in the literature than over his religious views. It is clear and generally accepted that his broad cultural aims included moderating the manners of a warrior caste and deflating the pretensions of any form of religious or ideological extremism based on claims to possess certain, transcendent truth of any kind. And although Montaigne does not endorse any constitutional form over any other (he would have appreciated Pope's couplet, in part "for forms of government, let fools contest"), there are characteristics of his thought which pull in the same direction as subsequent liberal democratic developments, saliently, the importance of a private realm and of the private conscience (though not necessarily to extend to religious dogma); the denigration of the public, political realm as a theater of alienating role-playing and instrumentality; a demand for public transparency insofar as possible; an aversion to cruelty of any sort; and a cultivation of the unique aspects of individual personality.

A recent book which makes a case for Montaigne as contributing to the rise of such "liberal" values is the aforementioned *Sensual Philosophy*. Levine sees Montaigne's individualism as different from subsequent individualisms (e.g., Lockean and Romantic) by virtue of its retention of classical restraints on the personality; and he sees Montaigne distanced from the classical political writers by virtue of the degree of subjectivity which he does allow. In brief, Levine sees Montaigne as providing a nuanced life plan for rare individuals with a clear perception of realistic requisites for human happiness, which has similarities to the kinds of liberalism grounded on skeptical premises (versus based on natural rights or "will") about the limits of human capacities in both knowledge and action.[41] A similar view is to be found in John Christian Laursen's *The Politics of Skepticism in the Ancients, Montaigne, Hume, and Kant*. Both Levine and Laursen distance themselves from the more extreme assertions of David Schaefer in *The Political Philosophy of Montaigne*, who argues that Montaigne is "one of the earliest advocates of the modern liberal regime" and "perhaps the original architect of what we know as "bourgeois morality," where "bourgeois" is taken to denote pacific, commercial habits in a tolerant society which elevate private over public pursuits.⁴² Let us look at some of Schaefer's assertions in this connection, in brief, that Montaigne had a grand, hidden, political project to attain a conditional immortality by transforming the views of both rulers and their civilizations, that is, by acting as a "legislator-founder" in the classical sense.

This is an interesting (if highly unlikely) thesis from the standpoint of our characterizations of Montaigne's art of living, for where our reading of the *Essais* suggested that whatever approximations of immortality in earthly life came in moments of fleeting delight in doing certain things for their own sake and eschewing whenever possible the realm of instrumental means, Schaefer proposes precisely the opposite. His reading of the *Essais* attempts to show that Montaigne sought a conditional, future earthly immortality through transformation of his civilization's fundamental values in the direction of the *ethos* now associated with bourgeois individualism, for example, through successful engagement in a practical, instrumental project of grand proportions.⁴³ In order to do this, Montaigne was required to mask his true aims through irony and even outright mendacity. Thus, in Schaefer's view, Montaigne's eschewal of mastery over others and of Machiavellianism and his profession of openness in communicating himself are not to be taken seriously in his own case (though they are for others as part of the new *ethos* he is propounding); rather Montaigne is engaging in a Machiavellian-like project suitable to his own position and talents and of future benefit to discerning persons like himself, and this is what Montaigne meant when he wrote that he tried to perform his public duties in as private a manner as possible—for example, to transform a civilization with the "hidden hand" rather than through ruling.⁴⁴

Let us look at some of Schaefer's other arguments in this connection. In my view, it is in the connections of his argument that he is overstated and hence inaccurate. That Montaigne saw the structure of political reality in terms similar to Machiavelli, and that his political values bear implicit structural similarities to those of modern liberalism, would seem beyond serious dispute. In a chapter devoted to Montaigne's "liberal politics," Schaefer adduces and analyzes text from the *Essais* to show that "fundamental tenets of classical political liberalism" are embodied in them: rights to individual security based on law, rights to freedom of worship and property, importance of individual conscience, of diversity, of chosen friendships, and so on.[45] By a much longer stretch of logical implication, Schaefer also attempts to show that Montaigne preferred that relations among individuals be governed by "the cash nexus" rather than ancestral or religious obligations.[46] (Schaefer is silent on Montaigne's undisguised admiration for the military art.) Except for this last point, and the issue of the *extent* to which Montaigne supported freedom of religious worship (and Schaefer might have added Montaigne's call for more public transparency), there are clear similarities with the subsequent classical liberal political *ethos* and program. But the reader of the *Essais* (and this book) must judge which way of looking at all this makes the more coherent sense of Montaigne's project. In my view Schaefer's speculations about Montaigne's hidden project are simply unnecessary to account for the evidence at hand. Montaigne had a preference for a life of repose through performance of ordinary acts done for their own sake as much as possible, an orientation made intellectually defensible by Christianity's view of the unity of body and soul, and its rejection of the classical dualist claim about the corruption inherent in matter. This, in turn, led him to a preference for private pursuits and relationships which allowed him to treat both persons and actions as ends rather than means instrumental to practical purposes. He stated (though one ironic effect of this elevation of the private would be to make the public realm more than ever a realm of instrumental means for securing the private realm) his views openly for the most part, in conformity with his own "ruling pattern" *(forme maistresse)*. If he were successful in influencing the political culture of his time, then so much the better. But he was clearly not prepared to pursue this practical aim at the alienated expense of denying his own personality, at the alienated expense of systematic and consistent dissimulation in the exploration and presentation of his own self. To have done so would have required someone like Machiavelli, who, as has been said, loved his country more than his own soul, and such a one was not Michel de Montaigne, who was prepared for the right cause to go to the edge of the fire, but not to jump in if he could avoid it.

Another recent argument in English to the effect that Montaigne can never be read at face value is to be found in the chapter on Montaigne in Alexander Nehemas, *The Art of Living: Socratic Reflections from Plato to Foucault*[47] (a work alluded to in our discussions of Montaigne's art of living in chapter 3). Based largely on an analysis of Montaigne's essay "On physiognomy," Nehemas attempts to show that, based on Montaigne's own reconstruction of the historic Socrates from inherited Platonic, Xenophonic, Ciceronian, and Plutarchian sources, Montaigne implies, among other things, that there is no assured correspondence between inner personality (given its changeability) and outer appearance and that the world of external appearance is so complex that great and time-consuming artiface and irony may be required to present an appearance of pure simplicity. In the cases of both Montaigne's Socrates and Montaigne, Nehemas argues by logical implication that great artifice was required to present the appearance of a natural purity; we should therefore never take either at face value. And in the account of the two threatening individuals who were disarmed by Montaigne's candor and openness (which story we reviewed in our account of "On physiognomy" in chapter 2), it was they who were likely the fools at judging Montaigne by his openness.[48]

In the case of Montaigne (the ironic Platonic Socrates is a different matter, for as an ontological dualist he could never have accepted the idea of mundane things done for their own sake), these arguments are highly unlikely given that, if true, they would have embroiled him in a realm of constant instrumentality. While it is true that Montaigne thought of the realm of appearances as contradictory and complex (as we saw in our comparisons with Rousseau), this was arguably precisely the reason he counseled himself to avoid acting in it whenever possible and why, in the essay "On physiognomy" (in a passage Nehemas does not mention), he says that we err in overestimating our abilities to control our fortunes and reputations:

> Nous faillons, ce me semble, en ce que nous ne nous fions pas assez au ciel de nous, et pretendons plus de nostre conduite qu'il ne nous appartient. Pourtant fourvoyent si souvent nos desseins.
>
> *We err, it seems to me, in that we do not trust ourselves enough to heaven, and expect more from our own conduct than belongs to us. That is why our plans often go astray.*[49]

On the issue of where Montaigne stood on the importance of military art and military honor or valor, James Supple, *Arms Versus Letters: The Military and Literary Ideals in the Essais of Montaigne*, is useful, though Supple is not at all concerned with refuting Schaefer's claim that Montaigne was the hidden craftsman of an incipient commercial, bourgeois *ethos*. (Supple is primarily concerned with the relative importance for

Montaigne of the military and literary humanist ideals in the education of the "nobility of the sword."] Sifting through text throughout the *Essais* as well as much secondary literature, Supple concludes that Montaigne's views on war and military life were complex, but that they can be successfully generalized about. He observes that though Montaigne's family could claim to be of the military aristocracy (having given up commercial trade for three generations except for the sale of estate wine); and although Montaigne may possibly have seen combat at close quarters and was clearly fascinated by classical instances of military valor in the face of death; still his view of war was that it was essentially an "illness," justifiable for self-defense of a nation, but not out of the kind of greed which drove European conquests of the new world:

> His attitude toward war is . . . finely balanced. Viewing it in the abstract, he sees war as an illness . . . which reduces rather than increases the stature of its participants. He . . . however . . . *offers no project of utopian reform*. He restricts himself to indicating when he believes that war is justified and when it is not . . . *he never waivers in his beliefs that one is justified in having recourse to arms to defend the established laws and religion of one's country*.[50]

As for Montaigne's fascination with military valor, Supple speculates that it stemmed from a more general desire to determine "the extent to which man can face up to the dangers and disasters of which life is so full."[51] At the very least, we can observe that Supple's discussion gives no support for Schaefer's claim that Montaigne preferred human association be based on the "cash nexus," and, in fact, Montaigne's critique of the greed-driven colonial conquests suggest reservations he would have had about them if they were somewhere made explicit to him as a future social possibility.

There has been obvious interest in Montaigne on the part of antifoundationist, postmodernist writers, given Montaigne's emphases on social role-playing, the limits of human knowledge, and his doubts about the consistency of his own self as he tries to know and observe it. In a sense, all such interpretation, including "participatory" readings of the meaning of texts, can be seen as extreme logical conclusions emanating from some of Montaigne's own sentiments about the changeability of himself from moment to moment (recall he does not paint himself but his passage), and his nominalist-like implications that only individual entities and instantaneous states exist. For overviews in English of this kind of antifoundationist Montaigne commentary, the reader might see the article by Richard

Regosin, "Recent Trends in Montaigne Scholarship: A Post-Structuralist Perspective,"[52] and the concluding chapter ("Montaigne Among the Postmoderns") of Dudley Marchi, *Montaigne Among the Moderns*.[53] For a good overview and critique of all approaches to Montaigne from neo-Nietzschean, Foucauldian, and Derridaen perspectives for failing to appreciate the sense of limits and the degree of (phenomenological) universality in Montaigne's subjectivism, see the fourth chapter of Alan Levine, *Sensual Philosophy*.[54]

In my view the general shortcomings (as interpretive Montaigne perspective) in this kind of antifoundationist, postmodernist literature[55] are two: (1) those which require the analysis of any text primarily from the standpoint of power relationships (including neo-Marxist as well neo-Nietzschean perspectives) can never grasp the centrality in his thought of Montaigne's insight about eschewing the world of instrumental means by living in the present moment, that is, doing things for their own sake; and (2) those which emphasize the instantaneous, discontinuous present to the exclusion of all else can never grasp the residue of sixteenth-century common sense and moral sensibility still so evident in Montaigne's (highly subjective) reflections on himself and his world. Additionally, these latter perspectives, when they go very far in deconstructing Montaigne's identity and the identity of his text, typically end up in the kind of neo-scholastic sterility and *ennui* attendant upon the exclusion of meaning from any text.

Concluding Postscript

This commentary has identified a unifying theme in the *Essais,* or at least a theme present throughout them, in early as well as late editions. This theme has been summarily indicated by the loosely intended phrase, "temporal solipsism," describing an orientation to live insofar as intelligently possible in the present moment, by structuring a life as fully as possible with activities appropriately done for their own sake and enjoyed in the very act of doing them. More instrumental activities directed toward future and uncertain ends are, in turn, minimized in such a life and, where unavoidable, performed in as "private" a manner as possible, even at risk of their practical failure. In achieving this outlook, we have seen Montaigne borrow ideas from various ancient writers and philosophic schools and combine them with his own version of Christianity to produce a unique synthesis of Greco-Roman, Christian, and Renaissance humanist ideas, all driven by, and forced to accommodate, Montaigne's own governing form *("forme maistresse")*.

We have also seen a recurring defense of Montaigne's own individuality (and, by implication, that of others as well) simply because it is his and his alone and not on the basis of any transcendental support for it of any kind. An interesting puzzle which occurs at this point is whether Montaigne's "temporal solipsism" is logically neccessitated by his individualism or vice-versa; whether they are at least logically consistent with one another and support one another; or whether they are simply contingently joined in Montaigne's personality. The first possibly cannot be right, for as is clear in the case of ancient *eudaimonian* philosophic schools, it is certainly possible to combine the desire to do and enjoy things for their own sake in the present moment, without being an individualist *à la* Montaigne. And the third possibility, while true, does not go far enough. Rather, the second possibility would seem the most accurate description of the relationship between "temporal solipsism" and individualism—they are logically consistent with one another and lend practical support to one another in a human life. The opportunities to value and cultivate one's uniqueness as an individual and to savor fleeting individual moments of consciousness are enhanced in a life devoted insofar as possible to avoiding instrumental projects and activities which threaten to efface one's individuality by submerging one in collective enterprises requiring constant effort and attention for future and uncertain benefits, in a life illuminated by the insight that the most certain path to human contentment lies in the direction of doing things for their own sake insofar as is prudently possible. This latter qualification—"insofar as is prudently possible"—is what distinguishes Montaigne's orientation toward doing things for their own sake in the present moment from *both* the ancient Pyrrhonian attempt to suspend judgment on all questions[1] and the attempt of certain Christian ascetic orders to abandon all concern for the future through complete submersion in God's will from minute to minute.[2] Montaigne's approach to psychic repose involves the use of at least some prudence in crafting and rescuing from the public realm private compartments well-suited for practices of "temporal solipsism" performed in moods of genuine candor and sincerity.

Notes

Chapter I: Introducing Montaigne and the Essais

1. See James J. Supple, *Arms Versus Letters: The Military and Literary Ideals in the"Essais" of Montaigne* (Oxford: Clarendon Press, 1984), 27–61, on the Montaigne family eligibility for inclusion in the *noblesse d'epée*.
2. Supple, *Arms Versus Letters*, 58.
3. For explanation of this convention, which goes back to the beginning of twentieth-century French Montaigne scholarship, see Donald M. Frame, *The Complete Essays of Montaigne* (Stanford: Stanford University Press, 1958), xvi.
4. For a postmodernist characterization of some postmodernist readings of Montaigne, and how they differ from more formal readings, see Richard L. Regosin, "Recent Trends in Montaigne Scholarship: A Post-Structuralist Perspective," *Renaissance Quarterly* 37 (Spring 1984): 34–54, especially 34–37; in these latter pages Regosin articulates a perspective challenging the formal, commonsensical view that "privileges" the idea that the essays can be evaluated against "a reality outside of the writing," including even the "self" which Montaigne portrays in the *Essais*.
5. I first presented this general viewpoint on Montaigne in an essay titled "Oakeshott and Montaigne: Individuality and Ritualistic Practice," in W. J. Coats, *Oakeshott and His Contemporaries* (Cranbury, N.J. and London: Associated University Presses, 2000), 15–27.
6. For representative instances from the Roman lyrical poet Horace, see his verse letters, "To Numicus, On How to Be Happy" and "To Maecenas, on Real Contentment," in Casper J. Kraemer, Jr., ed. *The Complete Works of Horace* (New York: Random House, 1936), 321–30. For a discussion of contextual differences in their respective views of leisure, see Michael O'Loughlin, *The Garlands of Repose* (Chicago: The University of Chicago Press, 1978), 235–87.
7. Rituals are human activities especially susceptible of being performed for their own sake, without conscious, extrinsic purpose; moreover, performing

more instrumental tasks in a ritualistic fashion makes them less instrumental. These points are developed in chapter 2 on Montaigne's "art of living."
8. Montaigne, *Oeuvres complètes* (Editions Gallimar, Bibliotheque de la Pleiade, 1962).
9. Montaigne, *Les Essais*, 3 Livres, 3rd ed, ed. Pierre Villey (Paris: Presses Universitaires de France, 1999).
10. See, for a representative instance in this connection, Donald M. Frame, *The Complete Essays of Montaigne*, II, 12, 457; and, more generally, chapter 3 on Montaigne's religious views.
11. For a discussion of this point, see M. B. Foster, *The Political Philosophies of Plato and Hegel* (Oxford, Clarendon Press, 1935).

Chapter II: Montaigne's Philosophy of Appropriate Living

1. Cited by Frieda S. Brown in *Religious and Political Conservatism in the Essais of Montaigne* (Geneva: Librarie Droz, 1963), 62. Brown notes that the Spanish envoy to Paris in 1588, Mendoza, sent a message to his king, which, in the French translation, said that Montaigne was generally held to be "un homme intelligent encore an peu brouillon." The original Spanish text is reproduced in Donald M. Frame, "New Light on Montaigne's Trip to Paris in 1588," *Romanic Review* 51 (1960): 172–73.
2. See, in particular, *First Corinthians*, 2, 14, any edition.
3. Aristotle, *Metaphysics*, Book 12, any edition.
4. Frame, 619–620, emphasis added; Villey, 816.
5. Frame, 612, emphasis added; Villey, 806.
6. Frame, 620, emphasis added; Villey, 816.
7. Frame, 704, emphasis added; Villey, 949.
8. Frame, 705, emphasis added; Villey, 923.
9. Frame, 705; Villey, 924.
10. Frame, 705, emphasis added; Villey, 924–25.
11. Frame, 706, emphasis added; Villey, 925.
12. Frame, 706, Villey, 928.
13. Frame, 715; Villey, 936. "Tout ainsi comme quand je debats contre un homme vigoureux je me plais d'anticiper ses conclusions, je luy oste la peine de s'interpreter, d'essaye de prevenir son imagination imparfaicte encores et naissante."
14. Frame, 136, emphasis added; Villey, 184.
15. Frame, 136, emphasis added; Villey, 184.
16. Frame, 137, emphasis added; Villey, 186. Montaigne does add that if a communion of souls were ever possible between marriage partners, it would exceed the kind of friendship he is describing with his friend, for it would engage the entire person. (He excludes homosexuality as "licentious.") Frame, 138.
17. Frame, 139, emphasis added; Villey, 188.
18. Frame, 140–141, emphasis added; Villey, 190.
19. Frame, 141, emphasis added; Villey, 190.
20. Frame, 141, emphasis added; Villey, 191.

21. Frame, 736, emphasis added; Villey, 964.
22. Frame, 425; Villey, 566.
23. Frame, 429, emphasis added; Villey, 569–70.
24. Frame, 244, emphasis added; Villey, 337.
25. Frame, 611, emphasis added; Villey, 805.
26. Frame, 611, emphasis added; Villey, 805.
27. Frame, 428, emphasis added; Villey, 569.
28. Frame, 243, emphasis added; Villey, 336–37.
29. Frame, 600, emphasis added; Villey, 791.
30. Frame, 601; Villey, 792. "Je suivray le bon party jusques au feu, mais exclusivement si je puis. Que Montaigne s'engouffre quant et la ruyne publique, si besoin est; mais, s'il n'est pas besoin, je scauray bon gré à la fortune qu'il se sauve...."
31. Frame, 601, emphasis added; Villey, 792.
32. Frame, 625, emphasis added; Villey, 824.
33. Frame, 626, emphasis added; Villey, 824.
34. Frame, 626, emphasis added; Villey, 825.
35. Frame, 626, emphasis added; Villey, 829.
36. Frame, 629, emphasis added; Villey, 829.
37. Frame, 629, emphasis added; Villey, 828–29.
38. Frame, 177, emphasis added; Villey, 240.
39. Frame, 177, emphasis added; Villey, 241.
40. Frame, 177; Villey, 241.
41. Frame, 175, emphasis added; Villey, 238.
42. Frame, 180; Villey, 245.
43. Frame, 180–81, emphasis added; Villey, 245.
44. Frame, 189–196; Villey, 258–267.
45. Frame, 190; Villey, 259. "Pourquoy, estimant un homme, l'estimez vous tout enveloppé et empacqueté: Il ne nous faict montre que de parties qui ne sont aucunement siennes, et nous cache celles par lesquelles seules on peut vrayement juger de son estimation."
46. Frame, 190, emphasis added; Villey, 260.
47. Frame, 193, emphasis added; Villey, 263.
48. Frame, 195, emphasis added; Villey, 266.
49. Frame, 196, emphasis added; Villey, 267.
50. Frame, 226, emphasis added; Villey, 312.
51. Frame, 55, emphasis added; Villey, 80.
52. Frame, 63, emphasis added; Villey, 91.
53. Frame, 227, emphasis added; Villey, 395.
54. Frame, 298; Villey, 410. "... pour declarer la mesure de ma veuë, non la mesure des choses."
55. Frame, 297, emphasis added; Villey, 409.
56. Frame, 297; Villey, 413. "... qui mesle un peu plus de fruit au plaisir...."
57. Frame, 300; Villey, 413. "... y est traictée à pieces décousues, qui ne demandent pas l'obligation d'un long travail, dequoy je suis incapable...."
58. Frame, 300; Villey, 414. "Je veux qu'uon commence par le dernier point...."
59. Frame, 311, emphasis added; Villey, 427.
60. Frame, 308, emphasis added; Villey, 424.

61. Frame, 308–309, emphasis added; Villey, 424.
62. Frame, 309, emphasis added; Villey, 425.
63. Frame, 309–0; emphasis added; Villey, 425.
64. Frame, 310; Villey, 425.
65. Frame, 472, emphasis added; Villey, 623–24.
66. Frame, 471, emphasis added; Villey, 622.
67. Frame, 474, emphasis added; Villey, 626.
68. Frame, 470; Villey, 620.
69. Frame, 480, emphasis added; Villey, 633–34.
70. Frame, 492, emphasis added; Villey, 648.
71. Frame, 488, Villey, 644.
72. Frame, 487, emphasis added; Villey, 643.
73. Frame, 499, emphasis added; Villey, 657.
74. Frame, 499, emphasis added; Villey, 657–58.
75. Frame, 504, emphasis added; Villey, 665.
76. Frame, 504, emphasis added; Villey, 665.
77. Frame, 504, emphasis added; Villey, 665.
78. Frame, 518; Villey, 684.
79. Frame, 518, emphasis added; Villey, 684.
80. Frame, 540; Villey, 715. "Il n'est passion qui esbranle tant la sincérité des jugemens que la colere."
81. Frame, 545, emphasis added; Villey, 720.
82. Frame, 554; Villey, 733.
83. Frame, 554, emphasis added; Villey, 733.
84. Frame, 554, emphasis added; Villey, 733.
85. On the general subject of Montaigne's admiration for military virtues, see James J. Supple, *Arms Versus Letters* (Oxford: Clarendon Press, 1984).
86. Frame, 633, emphasis added; Villey, 833.
87. Frame, 632, emphasis added; Villey, 833.
88. Frame, 633, emphasis added; Villey, 834.
89. Frame, 635, emphasis added; Villey, 836.
90. Frame, 635, emphasis added; Villey, 836.
91. Frame, 634–635, emphasis added; Villey, 835–86.
92. Frame, 681, emphasis added; Villey, 892.
93. Frame, 681, emphasis added; Villey, 892–93.
94. Frame, 681, emphasis added; Villey, 893.
95. Frame, 638; Villey, 841. "Je me deffens de la temperance comme j'ay faict autresfois de la volupté."
96. Frame, 639, emphasis added; Villey, 842. "Ma philosophie est en action, en usage naturel et present. . . ."
97. Frame, 693, emphasis added; Villey, 909.
98. Frame, 694, emphasis added; Villey, 909.
99. Frame, 694, emphasis added; Villey, 910.
100. Frame, 689, emphasis added; Villey, 903. ". . . toute art, jette sa fin hors d'elle: «nulla ars in se versatur». . . ."
101. Frame, 700, emphasis added; Villey, 917.
102. Frame, 688–689, emphasis added; 903.
103. Frame, 699–700, emphasis added; Villey, 916–17.

104. Frame, 701, emphasis added; Villey, 918. "La superiorité et inferiorité, ... sont obligées à une naturelle envie et contestation; il faut qu'elles s'entrepillent perpetuellement. Je ne crois ny l'une ny l'autre des droicts de sa compaigne: laissons en dire à la raison...."
105. Frame, 766, emphasis added; Villey, 1001.
106. Frame, 723, emphasis added; Villey, 948.
107. Frame, 729, emphasis added; Villey, 955.
108. Frame, 747, emphasis added; Villey, 978.
109. Frame, 769; Villey, 1007. "Qui ne vit aucunement a autruy, ne vit guere a soy."
110. Frame, 769; Villey, 1006. "... l'amitié que chacun se doibt."
111. Frame, 769–70, emphasis added; Villey, 1007.
112. Frame, 769, emphasis added; Villey, 1006.
113. Frame, 773–74, emphasis added; Villey, 1011–12.
114. Frame, 770, emphasis added; Villey, 1007.
115. Frame, 768, emphasis added; Villey, 1005.
116. Frame, 769, emphasis added; Villey, 1006.
117. Frame, 769, emphasis added; Villey, 1006.
118. Frame, 770, emphasis added; Villey, 1008.
119. Frame, 786, emphasis added; Villey, 1026.
120. Frame, 785, emphasis added; Villey, 1026.
121. Frame, 789, emphasis added; Villey, 1031.
122. Frame, 813, emphasis added; Villey, 1061.
123. Frame, 814; Villey, 1062.
124. Frame, 814, emphasis added; Villey, 1062.
125. For this interpretation, see Alexander Nehemas, *The Art of Living: Socratic Reflections from Plato to Foucault* (Berkeley: University of California Press, 1998), 103–27, who follows suggestions of Jean Starobinski. The problem with this interpretation is that not only would it make Montaigne a complete fraud (given his enthusiastic portrayal of candor as one of the essential elements of his personality), but it would embroil him constantly in the realm of instrumental means—a realm of thought and action not at all conducive to the tranquillity and repose he clearly seeks. The kinds of prudential subterfuge that Nehemas attributes to Montaigne are arguably more characteristic of the Platonic Socrates, who lived in a small, democratic city-state, without the privacy and anonymity Montaigne enjoyed in his familial estate under a sixteenth-century French monarchy.
126. Frame, 810, emphasis added; Villey, 1058.
127. Frame, 811; Villey, 1059.
128. In the title to Book I, Essay 27: "It is folly to measure the true and the false by our own capacity."
129. Frame, 812; Villey, 1060–61.
130. Frame, 812, emphasis added; Villey, 1061.
131. Frame, 852, emphasis added; Villey, 1110.
132. Frame, 853, emphasis added; Villey, 1111.
133. Frame, 853, emphasis added; Villey, 1112.
134. Frame, 851; Villey, 1108.
135. Frame, 851; Villey, 1108.

112 • MONTAIGNE'S ESSAIS

136. Jean Jacques Rousseau, *Social Contract*, Book I, chap. 1, any edition.
137. Arthur M. Melzer, *The Natural Goodness of Man* (Chicago: University of Chicago Press, 1990), 72. Emphasis added.
138. Melzer, *The Natural Goodness of Man*, 72. Emphasis added.
139. Melzer, *The Natural Goodness of Man*, 73. Emphasis added.
140. Melzer, *The Natural Goodness of Man*, 73. Emphasis added.
141. I simply refer to the obvious, as widespread availability of mobile telephones and electronic mail make it increasingly difficult ever to "get away from the office."
142. Michael Oakeshott, *Rationalism in Politics* (London: Methuen and Co. Ltd., 1962), 168. Emphasis added.
143. Oakeshott, *Rationalism in Politics*, 169. Emphasis added.
144. Quoted in Wendell J. Coats, Jr., *Oakeshott and His Contemporaries* (Cranbury, N.J. and London: Associated University Presses, 2000), 104. Emphasis added.
145. Oakeshott, *Rationalism in Politics*, 176.
146. Oakeshott, *Rationalism in Politics*, 146.
147. Oakeshott, *Rationalism in Politics*, 177–78. Emphasis added.
148. Oakeshott, *Rationalism in Politics*, 2–38.
149. See Coats, Jr., *Oakeshott and His Contemporaries*.
150. For development of this theme, see Charles Cochrane, *Christianity and Classical Culture* (Oxford: Oxford University Press, 1957), 447–85, especially 485: "to recognize that our nature and destiny are those of individuals, both here and here-after . . . a belief of supreme importance, for it means that there is nothing inherently fatal in matter."
151. Michael Oakeshott, *On Human Conduct* (Oxford: Clarendon Press, 1975), 236. Emphasis added.
152. Frame, 169, emphasis added; Villey, 229.
153. John Dewey, *Democracy and Education* (New York: Macmillan, 1966), 122. Emphasis added. See also Karl Marx, *The Grundrisse*, any edition.
154. This is a phrase of Michael Oakeshott, not used with specific reference to Montaigne.

Chapter III: Montaigne's Religious Views

1. Frame, 327, emphasis added; Villey, 448.
2. Frame, 321; Villey, 441.
3. Frame, 326, emphasis added; Villey, 446.
4. Sextus Empiricus, *Outlines of Pyrrhonism*, trans. R. G. Bury (Cambridge, Mass.: Harvard University Press, 1933), 21–93. For a lucid overview of the issues debated in the various, ancient skeptical schools, see John Christian Laursen, *The Politics of Skepticism in the Ancients, Montaigne, Hume and Kant* (Leiden: E.J. Brill, 1992), 1–93.
5. Frame, 331, emphasis added; Villey, 453.
6. Frame, 335, emphasis added; Villey, 458.
7. Frame, 336–337, emphasis added; Villey, 460.

Notes • 113

8. Frame, 339, emphasis added; Villey, 463.
9. Frame, 343, emphasis added; Villey, 468.
10. Frame, 345, emphasis added; Villey, 470.
11. Frame, 358; Villey, 486. "Et Dieu mesme . . . il faut qu'il y retire, comme nous dirons tantost."
12. Frame, 359, emphasis added; Villey, 488.
13. Frame, 363; Villey, 492. "Infinis esprits se treuvent ruinez par leur propre force et soupplesse."
14. Frame, 370; Villey, 500.
15. Frame, 370; Villey, 500. "Car, puis que le monde n'a point cogneu Dieu par sapience, il luy a pleu, par la vanité de la predication, sauver les croyans."
16. Frame, 370, emphasis added; Villey, 500. "Si me faut-il voir en fin s'il est en la puissance de l'homme de trouver ce qu'il cherche, et si cette queste . . . l'a enrichy . . . de quelque verité solide . . . Je croy qu'il me confessera, s'il parle en conscience, que tout l'acquest qu'il a retiré d'une si longue poursuite, c'est d'avoir appris à reconnoistre sa foiblesse."
17. Frame, 372, emphasis added; Villey, 503.
18. Frame, 373, emphasis added; Villey, 504.
19. Frame, 374; Villey, 505.
20. Frame, 375, emphasis added; Villey, 506.
21. Frame, 376; Villey, 507. ". . . pour y comparer la sienne et nous faire voir de combien il est allé plus outre et combien il a approché de plus pres la verisimilitude. . . . nous aprenons de luy que le beaucoup sçavoir aporte l'occasion de plus doubter.
22. Frame, 379, emphasis added; Villey, 511–12.
23. Frame, 380; Villey, 513.
24. Frame, 386, emphasis added; Villey, 520. "Elle ne fait que fourvoyer par tout, mais specialement quand elle se mesle des choses divines. . . . et qu-elle se destourne ou escarte de la voye tracée et battuë par l'Eglise, comme tout aussi tost elle se perd. . . ."
25. Frame, 389; Villey, 524.
26. Frame, 394; Villey, 529.
27. Frame, 394; Villey, 529.
28. Frame, 396, emphasis added; Villey, 531. "«*Profecto non Deum, quem cogitare non possunt, sed semet ipsos pro illo cogitantes, non illum sed se ipsos non illi sed sibi comparant*» . . ."
29. Frame, 408, emphasis added; Villey, 545.
30. Frame, 409; Villey, 546. ". . . un philosophe impremedité et fortuite!"
31. Frame, 415, emphasis added; Villey, 553.
32. Frame, 415, emphasis added; Villey, 554.
33. Frame, 423; Villey, 562. ". . . qu'il ne se void aucune proposition qui ne soit debatue et controverse entre nous. . . . qui est signe que je l'ay saisi par quelque autre moyen que par une naturelle puissance qui soit en moy et en tous les hommes."
34. Frame, 423, emphasis added; Villey, 563.
35. Frame, 424; Villey, 564. ". . . si Dien ne le reforme et fortifie par sa grace et faveur particuliere et supernaturelle."
36. Frame, 426, emphasis added; Villey, 566.

37. Frame, 428; Villey, 569–70. "Ainsi me suis-je, par la grace de Dieu, conserve entier, sans agitation et trouble de conscience, aux anciennes creances de nostre religion. . . ."
38. Frame, 437; Villey, 579. "Quelle verité que ces montaignes bornent, qui est mensonge au monde qui se tient au delà?"
39. Frame, 437; Villey, 579. ". . . sur l'eternelle base de sa saincte parolle!"
40. Frame, 447, emphasis added; Villey, 592. " . . . nous conclurrons, aux despens de ces deux grandes sectes dogmatistes, qu'il n'y a point de science."
41. Frame, 446, emphasis added; Villey, 590.
42. Frame, 454, emphasis added; Villey, 600–601.
43. Frame, 458, emphasis added; Villey, 602. ". . . et n'y a rien qui demeure ne qui soit tousjours un."
44. Frame, 457, emphasis added; Villey, 603.
45. Frame, 458, emphasis added; Villey, 604.
46. Blaise Pascal, *Pensées and Other Writings*, ed. Anthony Levi, trans. Honor Levi (Oxford: Oxford University Press, 1999), XXIV, 182–91.
47. Pascal, 188. Emphasis added.
48. Pascal, 188. Emphasis added.
49. Pascal, 188.
50. For a discussion of Montaigne's view of generalization, see Craig B. Brush, *Montaigne and Bayle* (The Hague: Martinus Nijhoff, 1966), 148.

Chapter IV: Montaigne's Political Views

1. Frame, 86; Villey, 119. For Montaigne, the word "innovation" *(nouvelleté)* meant essentially what we would call revolution or radical reform.
2. Frame, 87; Villey, 119.
3. Frame, 88, emphasis added; Villey, 121.
4. Frame, 89, emphasis added; Villey, 122.
5. Montaigne does not often cite scripture in support of his arguments, perhaps because this would be to imitate and encourage the Protestant conviction that each individual read and judge scripture for himself or herself.
6. Montaigne's reasoning here also has obvious similarities to Socrates' advice to philosophers to withdraw and turn away from the "storms" in their cities under certain conditions, in Plato, *The Republic*, Book VI, any edition.
7. Frame, 86, emphasis added; Villey, 118.
8. Frame, 821, emphasis added; Villey, 1072.
9. Frame, 600; Villey, 791.
10. Frame, 600; Villey, 791.
11. Frame, 600; Villey, 791.
12. Frame, 603; Villey, 794–95.
13. Frame, 601, emphasis added; Villey, 792.
14. Frame, 743, emphasis added; Villey, 973.
15. Frame, 142, emphasis added; Villey, 191.
16. Frame, 852, emphasis added; Villey, 1110.

17. Frame, 773–774, emphasis added; Villey, 1011–12.
18. See, in this connection, Donald Earl, *The Moral and Social Traditions of Rome* (Ithaca, N.Y.: Cornell University Press, 1967).
19. Frame, 428, emphasis added; Villey, 569.
20. John Christian Laursen, *The Politics of Skepticism in the Ancients, Montaigne, Hume, and Kant* (Leiden: E.J. Brill, 1992), 117.
21. Although Montaigne does say in an aside that democracy seems "the most natural and equitable form of rule." Frame, 12.
22. Frame, 611, emphasis added; Villey, 805.
23. Frame, 700–701, emphasis added; Villey, 917–18. (Although Lincoln had not read Montaigne, he echoes these sentiments in his famous quip that as he would not be a slave, so he would not be a master.)
24. Frame, 643, emphasis added; Villey, 846–47.
25. Frame, 677, emphasis added; Villey 887–88.
26. Frame, 678, emphasis added; Villey 889.
27. Frame, 681, emphasis added; Villey, 892–93.
28. Frame, 849, emphasis added; Villey, 1106.
29. It is interesting to reflect that perhaps Rousseau was driven in the "Discourse on the Origins of Inequality" to his dubious anthropological assumption about the isolated, individual existence of primitive human beings by his insight that "living in the present moment" was the natural impulse, rather than a laborious, ordered, social cooperation. This is an issue that Montaigne does not take up.
30. Frame, 153, emphasis added; Villey, 206.
31. Frame, 693, emphasis added; Villey, 908–9.
32. One of Tocqueville's central themes in *Democracy in America* concerns the danger to individual freedom of thought in the enormous pressures of majority opinion on the individual; Montesquieu's ideal type, "monarchie" (in *The Spirit of the Laws*) is more conducive to individual diversity than his ideal type "republique." For development of this latter theme in Montesquieu, see Michael Oakeshott, *On Human Conduct* (Oxford: Clarendon Press, 1975), 246–50.

Chapter V: Bibliographic Essay

1. Alan M. Boase, *The Fortunes of Montaigne: A History of The Essays in France, 1580–1669* (New York: Octagon Books, 1970). See, also, in this connection, Ian J. Winter, *Montaigne's Self-Portrait and Its Influence in France, 1580–1630* (Lexington, Ky.: French Forum Publishers, 1976).
2. For a depiction of Montaigne as a central figure in the sixteenth-century revival of ancient skepticism, and one of the creators of a new form of Fideism—Catholic Pyrrhonism, see Richard H. Popkin, *The History of Skepticism from Erasmus to Spinoza* (Berkeley: University of California Press, 1979, 52–65. On the differences between Montaigne and the ancient Skeptics, see John Christian Laursen, *The Politics of Skepticism in the Ancients, Montaigne, Hume and Kant* (Leiden: E.J. Brill, 1992), especially 123.

3. For a sustained account in English of Montaigne as a Fideist (one who believed that religious belief could not be founded on, or clarified by, reason), see Frieda S. Brown, *Religious and Political Conservatism in the Essais of Montaigne* (Geneva: Librarie Droz, 1963), who relies heavily on French sources, including the work of Herman Janssen on this topic. See, especially, Brown's important distinction in this connection in note #2, p. 43: "a division had been made by the church between revealed truths, such as the Trinity . . . and spiritual beliefs which included the existence of God. . . . *Montaigne's failure to make this distinction—to him neither category of beliefs was susceptible to reason—was what marks him as a fideist.*" (Emphasis added.) For another English language account of Montaigne as a Fideist, using skeptical argument in favor of his received religion, see Craig G. Brush, *Montaigne and Bayle: Variations on the Theme of Skepticism* (The Hague: Martinus Nijhoff, 1966), 35–159. For the view that Montaigne was neither a strict Pyrrhonian nor a Fideist, but a nondogmatic, atheistic, Academic Skeptic, see Alan Levine, *Sensual Philosophy* (Lanham, Md.: Lexington Books, 2001), 31–79.
4. For an analysis extracting Epicurean themes from the *Essais*, especially "the temporal indetermininancy of human experience," see Eric MacPhail, "Montaigne's New Epicureanism," *Montaigne Studies* 12 (Oct. 2000): 91–103.
5. Boase, *The Fortunes of Montaigne*, xxx. Emphasis added.
6. Boase, *The Fortunes of Montaigne*, xxx. Emphasis added.
7. Boase, *The Fortunes of Montaigne*, xxx. Emphasis added.
8. Boase, *The Fortunes of Montaigne*, xxxiii. Emphasis added.
9. Boase, *The Fortunes of Montaigne*, xxxiv. Emphasis added.
10. Donald M. Frame, *Montaigne: A Biography* (San Francisco: North Point Press, 1984).
11. Frame, *Montaigne: A Biography*, 148. Emphasis added.
12. Frame, *Montaigne: A Biography*, 298. Emphasis added.
13. Hugh Friedrich, *Montaigne*, ed. Philippe Desan, trans. Dawn Eng (Berkeley: University of California Press, 1991), 145.
14. Friedrich, *Montaigne*, 142. Emphasis added.
15. Friedrich, *Montaigne*, 142. Emphasis added.
16. Friedrich, *Montaigne*, 132. Emphasis added.
17. Friedrich, *Montaigne*, 132. Emphasis added.
18. Friedrich, *Montaigne*, 308. Emphasis added.
19. Tzvetan Todorov, *Imperfect Garden: The Legacy of Humanism*, trans. Carol Cosman (Princeton: Princeton University Press, 2002); Ann Hartle, *Michel de Montaigne: Accidental Philosopher* (Cambridge: Cambridge University Press, 2003).
20. "Certain aspects of his thought rank Montaigne in the humanist tradition; others suggest that he paved the way for individualism. His anthropology can be viewed as fundamentally humanist. He believes in the indeterminancy of human nature, which will be guided by custom but also by the 'voluntary freedom' of the subject. He knows that this nature is sociable. He does not forget, finally, that all men belong to the same species, and that this belonging weighs more heavily than national determination . . ." Todorov, *Imperfect Garden*, 166.

21. I have developed parallels between Montaigne and Oakeshott in *Oakeshott and His Contemporaies: Montaigne, St. Augustine, Hegel, et al.* (Cranbury, N.J. and London: Associated University Presses, 2000).
22. Todorov, *Imperfect Garden*, 166. Emphasis added.
23. Todorov, *Imperfect Garden*, 167. Emphasis added. See also, in this connection, Richard J. Quinones, *The Renaissance Discovery of Time* (Cambridge, Mass.: Harvard University Press, 1972), 241: "Montaigne transcends time by . . . sinking into the present."
24. Todorov, *Imperfect Garden*, 167.
25. See, for example, André Gide, *Montaigne*, trans. Dorothy Bussy (New York: McGraw-Hill, 1964), originally published 1939; and David Lewis Schaefer, *The Political Philosophy of Montaigne* (Ithaca, N.Y.: Cornell University Press, 1990).
26. See, for example, Alan Levine, *Sensual Philosophy* (Lanham, Md.: Lexington Brooks, 2001).
27. See, for example, Frieda S. Brown, *Religious and Political Conservatism in the Essais of Montaigne* (Geneva: Librarie Droz, 1963).
28. Ann Hartle, "The Dialectic of Faith and Reason in *The Essays of Montaigne*," *Faith and Philosophy* 18 (July 2001): 323–36.
29. Hartle, "The Dialectic of Faith and Reason . . . ," 324.
30. Hartle, "The Dialectic of Faith and Reason . . . ," 324.
31. Hartle, "The Dialectic of Faith and Reason . . . ," 333. Emphasis added.
32. Brown, *Religious and Political Conservatism* . . . , 41. In her recent book, *Michel de Montaigne: Accidental Philosopher* (Cambridge: Cambridge University Press, 2003), Hartle does argue that Montaigne lived a life of Christian faith as he understood it (p. 122), and that he intimates the possibility of a Christian republic (p. 230).
33. Catherine Demure, "Montaigne: The Paradox and the Miracle—Structure and Meaning in 'The Apology for Raymond Sebond,'" *Yale French Studies* 64 (1983): 188–208.
34. Demure, "The Paradox and the Miracle . . . ," 203.
35. Levine, *Sensual Philosophy*, especially 31–88.
36. Levine, *Sensual Philosophy*, 69. Emphasis added.
37. Levine, *Sensual Philosophy*, 69. Emphasis added.
38. Malcolm Smith, *Montaigne and the Roman Censors* (Geneva: Librarie Droz, 1981).
39. Smith, *Montaigne and the Roman Censors*, 109. Emphasis added.
40. Smith, *Montaigne and the Roman Censors*, 73. Emphasis added.
41. Levine, *Sensual Philosophy*, 167–200.
42. Schaefer, *The Political Philosophy of Montaigne*, 375 and 340. Laursen, *The Politics of Skepticism*, devotes nine full pages (131–39) to problems with Schaefer's ironic interpretation, which hinges on the difficulty of deciding which are (and which not) the unironic assertions. Levine, throughout *Sensual Philosophy*, is generally critical of Schaefer's failure to see the classically inherited limits to Montaigne's conceptions of liberty and self, limits not consistent with the subsequent, expansive bourgeois ideology.
43. Schaefer, *The Political Philosophy of Montaigne*, 37.

44. This phrase ("la main cachée) and strategy are typical of Rousseau's approach both to governing and child-rearing in the *Social Contract* and the *Émile*, respectively.
45. Schaefer, *The Political Philosophy of Montaigne*, 376.
46. Schaefer, *The Political Philosophy of Montaigne*, 376.
47. Alexander Nehemas, *The Art of Living: Socratic Reflections from Plato to Foucault* (Berkeley: University of California Press, 1998), 101–27.
48. Nehemas, *The Art of Living*, 126: "Montaigne's two enemies, who let him go on the basis of his honest face, may have been fools. Physiognomy cannot be trusted, especially when one, like Montaigne, is still in the process of fashioning himself."
49. Frame, 812, emphasis added; Villey, 1061.
50. James. J. Supple, *Arms Versus Letters: The Military and Literary Ideals in the 'Essais' of Montaigne* (Oxford: Clarendon Press, 1984), 257–58. Emphasis added.
51. Supple, *Arms Versus Letters*, 206.
52. Richard Regosin, "Recent Trends in Montaigne Scholarship: A Post-structuralist Perspective," *Renaissance Quarterly* 37 (Spring 1994): 34–54.
53. Dudley M. Marchi, *Montaigne Among the Moderns: Receptions of the Essais* (Providence, R.I.: Berghahn Books, 1994), 278–317. Marchi also has some interesting reflections (pp. 64–66) on Montaigne, Rousseau, and the attempt to live in the present moment.
54. Levine, *Sensual Philosophy*, 184–86, 234–40.
55. One of the more interesting anti-foundationist, postmodernist discourses to draw on Montaigne as a point of departure is to be found in Jacques Derrida, "Force of Law: The Mystical Foundation of Authority," trans. Mary Quaintance, *Cardoza Law Review* 11 (July–August 1990): 921–1045, esp. 937–45.

Concluding Postscript

1. In my view, Montaigne's relentless curiosity implies dramatically that pure Pyrrhonism generates more frustration than repose.
2. See, for example, the seventeenth-century work, *Abandonment to Divine Providence*, by Jean-Pierre de Caussade, trans. John Beavers (Garden City, N.Y.: Image Books, 1975), especially chap. 2: "Embrace the present moment as an ever-flowing source of holiness" (pp. 36–58). I've also suggested that Montaigne's attempt to live in the present moment differs from the classical Rationalist attempt to approximate divine stasis through philosophic contemplation. Although one might argue by implication that Montaigne's orientation does implicitly attempt an approximation to the activity of the creator God of Judeo-Christianity, since it is arguably only in ritual and in a ritualistic approach to mundane life that human beings can do things solely for their own sake or can momentarily be creators *ex nihilo*.

Bibliography

Boase, Alan. *The Fortunes of Montaigne: A History of the Essays in France, 1580–1609.* New York: Octagon Books, 1970.
Brown, Frieda S. *Religious and Political Conservatism in the Essais of Montaigne.* Geneva: Librarie Droz, 1963.
Brush, Craig B. *Montaigne and Bayle: Variations on the Theme of Skepticism.* The Hague: Martinus Nijhoff, 1966.
Caussade, Jean-Pierre de. *Abandonment to Divine Providence.* Trans. John Beavers. Garden City, N.Y.: Image Books, 1975.
Coats, Wendell J., Jr. *Oakeshott and His Contemporaries: Montaigne, St. Augustine, Hegel, et al.* Cranbury, N.J. and London: Associated University Presses, 2000.
Cochrane, Charles. *Christianity and Classical Culture.* London: Oxford University Press, 1957.
Demure, Catherine. "Montaigne: The Paradox and the Miracle—Structure and Meaning in 'The Apology for Raymond Sebond.'" *Yale French Studies* 64 (1983), 188–208.
Derrida, Jacques. "Force of Law: 'The Mystical Foundation of Authority.'" Trans. Mary Quaintance, *Cardoza Law Review* 11 (5–6) (July–August 1990), 919–1045.
Dewey, John. *Democracy and Education.* New York: Macmillan, 1966.
Earl, Donald. *Moral and Political Traditions of Rome.* Ithaca, N.Y.: Cornell University Press, 1967.
Emerson, Ralph Waldo. "Montaigne; or the Skeptic," in *Essays and Lectures.* New York: Library Classics of the United States, 1983, 690–709.
Foster, M. B. *The Political Philosophies of Plato and Hegel.* Oxford: Oxford University Press, 1935.
Frame, Donald M. *Montaigne: A Biography.* New York: Harcourt, Brace and World, 1965.

Friedrich, Hugo. *Montaigne*. Ed. Philippe Desan, trans. Dawn Eng. Berkeley: University of California Press, 1991.

Gide, André. *Montaigne*. Trans. Dorothy Bussy. New York: McGraw-Hill, 1964.

Hartle, Ann. "The Dialectic of Faith and Reason in *The Essays of Montaigne*." *Faith and Philosophy* 18. No. 3, July 2001, 323–35.

———. *Michel de Montaigne: Accidental Philosopher*. Cambridge: Cambridge University Press, 2003.

———. "Montaigne's Accidental Moral Philosophy." *Philosophy and Literature* 24, 2000, 138–53.

Horace. *The Complete Works of Horace*. Ed. Casper J. Kraemer. New York: Modern Library, 1936.

Laursen, John Christian. *The Politics of Skepticism in the Ancients, Montaigne, Hume, and Kant*. Leiden: E.J. Brill, 1992.

Levine, Alan. *Sensual Philosophy: Toleration, Skepticism, and Montaigne's Politics of the Self*. Lanham, Md.: Lexington Books, 2001.

MacPhail, Eric. "Montaigne's New Epicureanism," *Montaigne Studies* XII, Nos. 1–2, 2000, 91–103.

Marchi, Dudley. *Montaigne Among the Moderns*. Providence, R.I.: Berghahn Books, 1994.

McGowan, Margaret. *Montaigne's Deceits: The Art of Persuasion in the Essais*. Philadelphia: Temple University Press, 1974.

Melzer, Arthur M. *The Natural Goodness of Man: On the System of Rousseau's Thought*. Chicago: University of Chicago Press, 1990.

Montaigne, Michel de. *Les Essais*. 3 Livres, 3rd ed. Ed. Pierre Villey. Paris: Presses Universitaires de France, 1999.

———. *Oeuvres completes*. Paris: Editions Gallimar, Bibliotheque de la Pleiade, 1962.

———. *The Complete Essays of Montaigne*. Trans. Donald M. Frame. Stanford: Stanford University Press, 1958.

———. *The Complete Works of Montaigne*. Trans. Donald M. Frame. Stanford: Stanford University Press, 1957.

Nehemas, Alexander. *The Art of Living: Socratic Reflections from Plato to Foucault*. Berkeley: University of California Press, 1998.

Oakeshott, Michael. *On Human Conduct*. Oxford: Clarendon Press, 1975.

———. *Rationalism in Politics and Other Essays*. London: Methuen and Co., 1962.

O'Loughlin, Michael. *The Garlands of Repose: The Literary Celebration of Civic and Retired Leisure*. Chicago: University of Chicago Press, 1978.

Pascal, Blaise. *Pensées and Other Writings*. Ed. Anthony Levi, trans. Honor Levi. Oxford: Oxford University Press, 1999.

Popkin, Richard. *The History of Skepticism from Erasmus to Spinoza*. Los Angeles: University of California Press, 1985.

Quinones, Ricardo J. *The Renaissance Discovery of Time*. Cambridge, Mass.: Harvard University Press, 1972.

Quint, David. *Montaigne and the Quality of Mercy: Ethical and Political Themes in the Essais*. Princeton: Princeton University Press, 1998.
Regosin, Richard. "Recent Trends in Montaigne Scholarship: A Post-Structuralist Perspective." *Renaissance Quarterly* 37 (1984), 34–54.
Rousseau, Jean-Jacques. *The First and Second Discourses*. Ed. and trans. Roger D. Masters. New York: St. Martin's Press, 1964.
———. *The Social Contract and Discourses*. Trans. G.D.H. Cole. London: J.M. Dent and Sons, Ltd., 1973.
Schaefer, David Lewis. *The Political Philosophy of Montaigne*. Ithaca, N.Y.: Cornell University Press, 1990.
Sextus Empiricus. *Outlines of Pyrrhonism*. Trans. R. G. Bury. Cambridge, Mass.: Harvard University Press, 2000.
Smith, Malcolm. *Montaigne and the Roman Censors*. Geneva: Librarie Droz, 1981.
Starobinski, Jean. *Montaigne in Motion*. Trans. Arthur Goldhammer. Chicago: University of Chicago Press, 1985.
Supple, James, J. *Arms Versus Letters: The Military and Literary Ideals in the "Essais" of Montaigne*. Oxford: Clarendon Press, 1984.
Todorov, Tzvetan. *Imperfect Garden: The Legacy of Humanism*. Trans. Carol Cosman. Princeton: Princeton University Press, 2002.
Ward, Keith. *God: A Guide for the Perplexed*. Oxford: One World Publications, 2002.
Winter, Ian. *Montaigne's Self-Portrait and Its Influence in France, 1580–1630*. Lexington, Ky.: French Forum Publishers, 1976.

Index

Academic Skeptics, 4, 6, 66
Alexander, 51, 58
anger, 36
antifoundationalism, 103, 104
Appolo, 73
appropriate living, 57
Aristotle, 11, 55, 66, 67, 68, 69, 70
Arms Versus Letters: The Military and Literary Ideals in the Essais of Montaigne (Supple), 102
"art of living," 4, 33, 50, 51, 57, 91, 94, 100
Art of Living: Socratic Reflections from Plato to Foucault (Nehemas), 101
authority of law, 81

Boase, A., 90
Boétie, E. de la, 1
Brown, F., 96

Cato the younger, 30, 31, 56, 58
Charrron, P., 90
Chrysippus, 70
Cicero, 29
classical dualism, 55
common friendship, 15
conceptions of God, 61
confrerer, 13
conversation, 13–15
conversative disposition, 53
Cyneus, 26

Democracy and Education (Dewey), 56
Demure, C., 97
Descartes, R., 7, 90
Dewey, J., 55, 56, 57
diversion, 38
dogmatic philosophy, 69–70
dogmatists, 67

Epicureans, 66, 73
Epicurus, 68
equipollent opposition, 18
Erasmus, 93
Essais (Montaigne), 1
  anger and, 36
  "Apology for Raymond Sebond," 2, 3, 7, 60
  "art of living" and, 4, 33, 50, 51
  description of, 2
  European colonialism and, 41, 88, 89
  Frame translation of, 1
  French editions of, 7
  human contentment and, 9–10, 11
  human psychic harmony and, 11, 12
  human reasoning and, 5
  individuality and, 5, 55
  interpretation of, 3–4
  Pleiade edition of, 7
  secondary literature on, 90
  vanity and, 42–44
  view of self, 13

Essais (continued)
   Villey edition of, 7
   Also see Montaigne, M. de
eudaimonian schools of thought, 10, 11
European colonialism, 41, 88, 89

fatherhood, 28
forme maistresse, 6, 10, 56, 57, 101, 105
Fortunes of Montaigne: A History of the Essays in France, 1580–1669 (Boase), 90
Frame, D. M., 91
Friedrich, H., 92
friendship, 15–16

Gide, A., 95
Gournay, M. de, 90

Hartle, A., 93, 94, 95, 96
Henry IV (Henry of Navarre), 1
Hiero, 25
Hobbs, T., 51
Horace, 6, 25, 94
human knowledge, 64, 65, 71, 73, 86
human reasoning, 5, 72–73
human reality, 18
human vanity, 64
Hume, J., 7, 94

ignorance, 27–28
Imperfect Garden: The Legacy of Humanism (Todorov), 93
individuality, 5, 55, 82, 99

Julius Caesar, 37, 51

Kant, E., 7

La Fontaine, J. de la, 90
La Rochefoucauld, M., 90
Laursen, J. C., 99
Levine, A., 95, 97, 99, 104

Machiavelli, 33
Marchi, D., 104
Margaret of Valois, 60
Marx, K., 55, 56, 57
master form, 58

Melzer, A., 52
Michel de Montaigne: Accidental Philosopher (Hartle), 93
Moliére, 90
Montaigne (Friedrich), 92
Montaigne: A Biography (Frame), 91
Montaigne Among the Moderns (Marchi), 104
Montaigne and the Roman Censors (Smith), 98
Montaigne, M. de, 1
   art of living and, 4, 33, 50, 51, 57, 91, 94, 100
   as mayor of Bordeaux, 1
   belief in openness, 47–48
   conversation and, 13–15
   democratic cultures and, 8
   democratic viewpoints of, 87
   diversion and, 38–39
   Erasmus and, 93
   fatherhood and, 28
   friendship and, 15–16
   happiness and, 27
   human reality and, 18
   human reasoning and, 5
   ignorance and, 27–28
   John Dewey and, 55–56
   life of great kings and, 42
   military ideals and, 102–103
   on obligations to others, 44–45
   on punishment of crime, 47
   political ambition and, 37, 99
   political views of, 79–89
   power, status, and, 52
   preference for private life, 19–21, 22–23, 35, 45–46, 50–51, 82, 83, 105
   public officials and, 25–26
   religion and, 56, 60–78
   St. Augustine and, 4
   self and, 18–19
   self-worth and, 33–34
   senses and, 73–74
   sex and, 21, 39–40
   theater roles, gaming, and, 84
   vanity and, 76
   view of books, 21–22, 28
   virtue and, 29–32
   Also see Essais

Montesquieu, Baron de, 89

Natural Goodness of Man (Melzer), 52
nature of the divinity, 69
Nehemas, A., 101, 102
Nietzsche, F., 5, 59
noblesse d'epée, 1

Oakeshott, M., 6, 51, 53, 54, 55, 94
Occam, W. de, 94
ontological dualism, 74
Outlines of Pyrrhonism, 62

Pascal, B., 10, 75, 76, 90
Pauline Christianity, 10
Pensées, 75
Peripatetics, 66
philosophic knowledge, 65
Plato, 55, 58, 68, 69, 70
Plutarch, 6, 29
Political Philosophy of Montaigne (Schaefer), 99, 100
Politics of Skepticism in the Ancients, Montaigne, Hume and Kant (Laursen), 99
Pope, A., 99
postmodernism, 103, 104
Protestantism, 80
psychic harmony, 11
psychikos, 10
Pythagoras, 68
Pyrrho, 6, 66
Pyrrhus, 26
Pyrrhonian Skeptics, 4, 6, 86

Rationalism, 95
Regosin, R., 104
rituals, 24, 85
Romanticism, 16

Rousseau, J.-J., 6, 7, 22, 42, 51, 52, 82

St. Augustine, 4, 8, 55, 58, 69, 81
St. Paul, 10, 68, 69, 81
St. Thomas Aquinas, 77
Schaefer, D., 99, 101, 103
Sebond, R., 2, 3, 7, 60, 61
self, 18–19
self-devotion, 34–35
selfless friendship, 15
self-worth, 33–34
Seneca, 5, 6, 29, 94
Sensual Philosophy (Levine), 97, 99, 104
sex, 21, 39–40
Sextus Empiricus, 62, 91
Skeptics, 58, 62, 66
Smith, M., 98
Social Contract, 51
Socrates, 30, 31, 48, 49, 58, 65, 102
Stoics, 58, 66, 73
subjectivity, 92
Supple, J., 102, 103

teleological thinking, 11
temporal solipsism, 24, 49–50, 105
Thales, 70
Theoria, 55, 59
Tocqueville, Baron de, 89
Todorov, T., 93, 94

Villey, P., 90
vanity, 42–44
Vico, G., 94
virtue, 29–32

willful subjectivity, 93

Xenophon, 25, 58